A Year and a Day

On Just a Few Acres

Peter Larson

buck buck books

For Hilarie

Introduction

Despite the pots into which pollsters and marketers divide us, each of us is a wonderfully unique mix of technician and dreamer, doer and thinker. Very few of us exist solely on one side of any line. Creativity informs practicality. Science informs art. To exist on one or the other side of a duality is to live without color or shade; in black or white. It is an illness of our modern age. The line is the creation of those who would tell us what we should be, how we should consume, and what success is.

This book is about my journey toward light and beauty. These occupy neither one side nor the other of any line. I am writing about poetry and mechanics, together. One may read it and appreciate the simple beauty of everyday tasks. Another may read it and see the poetic beauty - the higher meaning - I drew from those everyday tasks. I ask you to respect both. And most of all, I ask you to discount neither.

A life of wholeness exists in both abstraction and

practicality; looking up and looking down, secularity and spirituality. It took me 45 years to become comfortable in my own skin, to realize there was no fault in my attraction to both. Still I carry a deserved disrespect for those who care about only one or the other. This may be my fault, but I will stand that its endemic nature in today's society is one of our fateful ills.

I was born of a place, and my denial of that place, my denial of who I was born to be, gnawed at my subconscious for twenty years before I allowed these other selves to experience the light through my eyes. Once I allowed such, I became whole. My destiny crossed society's contract; led me to step off the treadmill I had been placed on in grade school. This leap took uncommon courage. I will forever be proud of it and I wish it for you.

I do not believe my case is unique. There are many out there in the big buildings, in the shopping malls, in the placeless businesses, wondering what is missing and not quite able to take a leap. I had the privilege, and maybe the naïveté, to take that leap. I hope the example of my experience may help in some small way. I needed a connection to something real; I needed to *produce* something tangible. At the same time, I needed to know the psychological and the spiritual dimensions of my work. The office cubicle offered little beyond the papers on the desktop and the internet's impenetrable window on the world. I felt trapped.

This book is about my discovery of myself. It is about my reconnection to my family's heritage. It is about the past and the future. I am proud to be the seventh generation on my family's farm, and that I am farming this land as it has not been farmed before. I am proud of farming as a creative and improvisational endeavor. I am proud to respect my heritage while adapting our land to what our future requires.

Within this book you will find a mixture of the pragmatic and the poetic. I looked for meaning in everyday tasks, and their relationship to my spirituality. I looked for common themes with the philosophies I developed in my previous life as an architect, centered around the industrial world's relationship with nature. Each chapter is a mixture of these things. Some of the chapters are introduced by essays in italics; I wrote these while I was an architect. They are included because they are pertinent to the subject of the chapter.

I am enthusiastic in my beliefs: if you feel a calling, follow it; if a leap must be taken, jump; if your heart beats for more than modernity, follow it. Progress is not progress if it doesn't stir your spirit. I found my way ahead through my past.

Pete Larson
born again farmer

One

Memory, of course, is a product of time. But memory is distinct from time in that it weights certain experiences. Time is a river, and we float down its steady current. Memory is not the river itself; it is the islands passed and explored, the changing landscape of the shores and the breath caught as new vistas are revealed at each bend. Memory is not linear as the river was/is/will be; memory is nodal, like the bright centers and fading arms of galaxies. And the vast black spaces between.

*   *   *

Quiet, darkness, family sleeping, children bright souls. I woke at 3am and tried to be still next to Hilarie while my mind wandered the remaining hours. At 6am I rose and walked the path I knew step by step in the darkness down to the kitchen, to a halo over the kitchen sink and clothes placed in the adjacent mudroom the night before.

After dressing, I continued out into the twenty degree December darkness to walk downward across the big field of soybean stubble to the tree stand, barely seen in the dim hedgerow, again guided by my footsteps' memory.

I climbed into the high stand with my shotgun slung over my shoulder, brushed the thin coat of snow off the seat and sat. I put my coffee thermos on the foot rest. I dug my second pair of rag gloves out of my coat pocket and pulled them on over my thin windproof pair. It was still dark and the moon had set. There was only a single hazy planet in the cloudy western sky.

There was no wind, there was no sound. Such silence made audible the high-pitched whine in my ears, reminded me of their function, although there was nothing to be heard. I should hold my breath; my violation of the calm would mark me a trespasser. The silence pulled my being into the dim.

*   *   *

I leaned my forehead on the side window and drifted in and out of sleep. The car sped down the interstate through the blue rain of evening. Water smacked the windshield; drops skated the length of the side windows and were thrown off the wheels into a vapor trail behind. The driver was talking work with the passenger up front.

I was in the car and not; alone some place beyond.

Tonight I would be the show, a big fish in a small pond, responsible for stretching and moving a large group of people in a common direction.

The car parked behind a large old building where the meeting would be held. It was dark now. I rubbed my eyes, got out of the car, stretched, and swapped my coat for a blazer. The rain had become a drizzle. We went up into the building's large hall, shook the hands of the other attendees and smiled, made small talk and sat in folding chairs to wait for the meeting to begin. I felt the mood of the room, looked at the people in charge and guessed what they expected of me, listened carefully to those who spoke before my turn and gauged the reactions of the room.

When it was my turn, I stood up and fell into myself, gathered the entire room and held it in my hand. In the next half hour I took them from where they were, drew them together and showed them the sense and spirit of a wonderful new place they each could almost see and touch. I was a success.

I rode home half asleep, in despair of the next day, week, month, year.

*   *   *

5:30am and so much to do. While Hilarie and the children slept, I quietly stepped the way from our bedroom on the second floor down to the mudroom. I put on the ragged shorts and T shirt I had left there the night before. Pulled on knee-high rubber barn boots over my socks to keep my feet dry in the heavy morning dew. Filled a bottle of water from the mudroom sink to drink on my way. I was out in time to see the sun rise; good weather today.

The chickens were always the first awake. Out in the pasture behind the house, the meat birds were telling me about their hunger. I stopped on my way to open the nesting boxes of the laying chickens; they would lay most of their eggs by mid-morning. One by one I moved the ten foot by twelve foot by two foot high open-bottomed pasture boxes, each containing fifty broiler chickens, four boxes total; then two boxes containing the laying chickens and the young turkeys. I moved the boxes by first inserting a wheeled dolly that lifted one end, then lifting the other end by holding its wire and garden hose loop and pulling it forward by hand. Each box was moved ahead one length every morning to give its inhabitants access to new pasture. Each box's trail was a series of rectangles of manure and trampled grass, each representing a day. Ten box-days back down the trail it tapered into bright green pasture grasses, fed with the chickens' droppings and aerated by their scratching.

I filled the feed trough in each box from bright silver galvanized trash cans that stored feed from the local mill, four cans in a row, holding 100 pounds each. As each was emptied it leapfrogged the pasture boxes to its next spot down the line, to where the boxes would be in a week or so. Then I filled each box's five gallon water bucket from the long network of garden hoses that snaked across the pasture.

The meat chickens attacked their feed, climbing over each other and squawking with beaks full of cracked corn, oats, and soybeans. This ruckus would last about an hour until the trough was pecked clean. Sometimes we could hear from the house's yard when these last bits of feed were being eaten, as a rapid t-t-t-t-t-t-t-t-t of beaks pecked bits from the metal bottoms of the troughs. Afterwards, the chickens would lay in the sun with bulging crops at the base of their necks, metering feed through their digestive tract and down to their gizzards to be ground by the small stones they had eaten. The laying chickens and turkeys were much mellower than the meat chickens about their feed situation, more interested in laying their morning eggs or investigating the new grass under their feet.

I sat on the corner of one of the pasture boxes to watch the sun rise, filtered through the leaves of the walnut trees around the house. Our farm is a big square shape, 45 acres in all. The land slopes gently downhill from the east to the west, toward Cayuga Lake. We could not see the lake from the farm; it was too far below us. But we could see the land rising up from its opposite shore.

At 38 miles, Cayuga is the longest of the Finger Lakes of central New York. It is 3½ miles across at its widest point, and was as deep as 435 feet. The Native American Iroquois Confederacy coined the name Finger Lakes, long before Europeans arrived. It is a collection of long, thin lakes, that when seen on a map, look like a giant hand had made its print on the landscape. They were formed by the advance and retreat of glaciers during the last ice age. The lakes varied greatly in size, with smaller lakes on either side of the "hand," and the largest lakes, Cayuga and Seneca, in the middle.

Between the lakes, which range from 5 to 20 miles apart, the land rises steeply from one then down to the next. We lived near the top of the slope on the east side of Cayuga Lake. Just above us the land began sloping toward the east and Owasco Lake. Creeks had carved many beautiful gorges and waterfalls into the hills around the lakes, the land was some of the most fertile in New York, and the slopes and moderating effect of lakes on the weather resulted in the success of many wineries and orchards in the region.

Ithaca lies at the south end of Cayuga Lake, and our farm is in Lansing, north of Ithaca. Ithaca is the home of Cornell University and Ithaca College. It is a progressive city, largely due to the influence of the faculty and students of these institutions. It is culturally rich beyond its small population of 30,000; with a wide variety of arts, music, and food. And it is also a hotbed of locally grown food and sustainable living. Driving around Ithaca, you would think it was where the bumper sticker was first invented, because the locals' cars are covered with them:

> Ithaca is gorges
> No farms no food
> Ithaca: 10 square miles surrounded by reality
> Ithaca: 10 square miles surrounded by farms

The winters are cold, the skies are often cloudy, and the summers are often HH&H (hot, hazy, and humid). But this area's rolling hills and deep green summers are the most beautiful I know. Except for the usual teenage desire to escape small town life, I never had any desire to live anywhere else.

Roads border the east and north sides of our property. Our house is near the intersection of those roads, a Greek Revival farmhouse built in the mid-1800's, similar to many in this area of upstate New York. When Hilarie and I first moved back to the farm from the city, the house was a wreck, and we spent fifteen years restoring it. The house is surrounded by large black walnut trees. There is a three bay garage, workshop, and woodshed behind the house; a winter chicken house, and a large pole barn. The original timber-framed barns have long since passed. My parents live on a small parcel next door, carved from the farm's square when I was a kid and my grandfather lived in our house.

One bay of our garage holds two makeshift brooders, four foot by eight foot open-top plywood boxes with pine flake bedding over the concrete floor, each with a 250 watt heat lamp suspended above it by wire from the ceiling. Here, day-old chicks and turkeys arriving from the hatchery spend the first weeks of their lives. This day, there were 30 two week old turkey poults in one brooder, and the other brooder was empty, awaiting more cornish cross chicks in the mail. I fed and watered the poults.

The winter chicken house stands at the back corner of the garage. We had recently added a hoop house to the back of the original shed to expand our laying flock. Now it held about seventy layer pullets, older than chicks but not old enough to lay eggs yet, of about ten different breeds. Again, I fed and watered.

Lastly I moved on to our three pigs in their pasture behind the pole barn, still sleeping in their little shelter, which I had been told looked a lot like the mangers built in front of churches at Christmas time. I opened the gate, and with a pail of feed in hand, stepped over the low electric fence wires into their pasture. The chase was on. I headed to their trough and they trailed me closing the gap. The trick was to get the feed in the trough before the pigs arrived, otherwise they nosed the bucket and feed spilled all over the ground. This time I beat them to the trough. Then I went back through the gate to get a pail of water, and back in to fill their drinking trough, made from the cut-off bottom of a vinegar barrel. It was 7:30, morning chores were done and it was time for breakfast.

Breakfast was simple, the same every day. A banana and honey cakes: Hilarie's homemade concoction of rolled oats, peanut butter, honey, and milk powder rolled into golf ball size cakes. Like Tolkien's elvish way bread, five of these calorie-dense balls carried me through to lunch. Hilarie was drinking her coffee, standing at the kitchen counter working on serving our three kids their waffle breakfast, prepared and frozen a few times per week. After eating, I filled my coffee cup and headed back out to work in the vegetable garden before it got too hot.

The vegetable garden is behind the house at the edge of the pasture, past a row of lilac and weigela bushes. It has a fence made of black locust posts and four-foot high welded wire mesh, buried a foot deep to keep the woodchucks out. Entrance is through a cedar gate with an arbor overhead, and the trumpet vines were in bloom. I pulled out three rows of arugula, mustard, and romaine that had bolted, and set them aside for the kids to feed to the laying hens later. I worked the soil with a skuffle hoe to prepare the ground for new greens and radishes. For us, greens were the staple of the garden, and we planted them every few weeks throughout the spring and summer.

Hilarie called from the back door of the house that the post office had called, to say our 100 chicks were there to be picked up (there was always a loveable peeping in the background of those calls). She would take the kids and pick them up as soon as the kids were dressed. I finished planting the greens and covered the rows with deer netting (to keep the mice and rabbits out), while she drove to town and back.

The kids piled out of the van and Hilarie walked around to open the passenger side door. She brought out two boxes lined with air holes, filled with peeping chicks. We brought them into the garage and set them next to the empty brooder. The kids always loved when we first opened the boxes to see what was inside. As they kneeled around, I pulled off the lid of the first and revealed twenty healthy yellow chicks. We counted them as we put each into the brooder. The second, larger box contained four chambers with twenty live chicks each, and two dead chicks. The hatchery always shipped a few extra, expecting some loss in transit. Newly hatched chicks can survive up to three days without food or water. Once they landed in the brooder, however, sustenance was not their priority. Heat was their first priority. They huddled together under the heat lamp until they felt comfortable at near 100 degrees. Then they ranged away to the food and water placed nearby. We watched the chicks for a while, then I headed back to the garden to weed. Grace, our six year old daughter, helped for a while, then wandered off to see if Grandma was home. Cora, our ten year old daughter, rode her bike up and down the back walk, and Henry, our five year old son, played in the "mudbox" (sand and water) near the winter coop.

By lunchtime, the garden was too hot to stay in no matter how acutely I tilted my wide-brimmed straw hat to block the sun. I had finished my work and the garden looked significantly neater than when I started. My garden housekeeping typically declined from July onward, especially this year with all the livestock to tend to. Every year, Hilarie took charge of the picking, canning, and freezing as my interest tapered off.

Lunch was usually catch-as-catch-can; whatever leftovers there were. Today it was summer squash quiche and plenty of water. I changed my shirt and sat under the dining room ceiling fan to eat, in no hurry to get back outside. Hilarie sat with me and ate a salad, and the kids watched TV in the front room. I was excited about a new way to efficiently build a turkey coop I had read about, and spent most of lunch talking to Hil about it, working through the details of how the parts would go together. Coop construction was this afternoon's job.

Although it was late July, I was thinking about winter and the animal stock we would be carrying through the cold weather. We had decided to try raising Bourbon Reds, a heritage breed of turkeys. Fifteen of the thirty turkeys in the garage brooder were Bourbon Reds, and the other fifteen were Broad Breasted Whites - typical Thanksgiving turkeys. In three weeks the whites would go to pasture, and would be ready for Thanksgiving. But we intended to raise the Bourbon Reds as a breeding flock, to sell meat, poults, and eggs from. This meant they would need their own house to winter in, which I planned on placing beside the existing winter chicken house.

We were constructing our farm shelters, fences, and other infrastructure to be portable, cheap, and adaptable. Our pasture boxes moved every day, and were screwed together so they could be taken apart, repaired, and modified as needed. Our turkeys ranged outside within electric net fencing after ten weeks of age, which was moved once per week around the pasture and was powered by a solar charger. I had built a hoop house addition for our expanding layer flock, bending salvaged chain link fence posts for the hoops and stretching a plastic covering over them to maximize light and solar heat.

For our winter turkey house, I was planning a simpler and cheaper structure, for which I had previously gathered the supplies, and started building that afternoon. Its base a rectangle of 2"x4" lumber, ten feet by sixteen feet. Its superstructure was four arched cattle panels bought at the farm store, heavy gauge welded wire mesh rectangles, each four feet high by sixteen feet long, and connected to the 2"x4" base with large hammer driven staples. The whole thing was covered with a 16 foot by 20 foot tarp, and the ends were made of 2"x3" framing and 3/8" plywood.

By 4:00pm it was time for afternoon chores. I had the turkey house constructed, except for the plywood and tarp skin. I had built it in the driveway in front of the workshop door, and as I had hoped, I could easily pick up one end to move it. With the pasture box dolly I could wheel it to its spot behind the garage.

Afternoon chores were a repeat of those in the morning, except the pasture boxes did not need to be moved. By 4:30 I was inside the house and took a shower. By 5:00 I was sitting in my favorite chair with my feet up on another in the dining room while Hilarie fixed dinner in the kitchen, which together formed one big space. Soon Henry and Grace were climbing on me; no nap this evening!

After a dinner of salad greens and chicken/vegetable fried rice, the kids and I laid on the dining room floor, one on my back and the other two to either side, watching me play video games on the tablet. At 7:00 it was time for the kids to start getting ready for bed. There were the usual complaints about tooth brushing, and Henry dragged his feet to his room as he always does. Hil read to Cora in her bedroom upstairs then to Henry in his small bedroom downstairs, while I read to Grace in her downstairs bedroom.

In our old house, each room held a family history.

Cora's was the room where my uncle and his girlfriend had stayed in the '70's after he came back from the service (and where he kept a large table for drying home-grown marijuana). But in the 19th century, it was my great great grandfather and grandmother's room, complete with feather bed. Cora still sleeps in that bed, with the feather tick replaced by a regular mattress. Grace's room was once the pantry, and after that our temporary kitchen until we built the present kitchen addition. And Henry's room was my great grandmother's bedroom, in fact the room she died in.

By 8:00 most (but not all!) of the kids' bedtime requests had been met. It was Hil mostly, who would walk back and forth from kitchen to each bedroom to respond to "more water," "I need a book," and "final tuck-in!" Hilarie and I sat at the kitchen island checking email and reading the newspaper while drinking beer and homemade wine. I played my guitar until about 9:30, and then we went upstairs to bed.

Two

I sat in my tree stand. The woods sighed with a slight breath of wind at sunrise.

The woods are connected to the hedgerows and the other woods. They feel as one; I feel its consciousness. Its language travels far distances, vibrations through the woods and the hedgerows around the fields. My grandfather died in the woods when I was a child. Afterwards, I was afraid of the woods and the hedgerows. They held his last energy; each tree knew what had happened, held the will he bore when he died. I waited for the woods to speak for him; I waited for something to say. It was not a child's fear.

The woods' boundary is not lightly violated. A wave travels through the woods as something enters, then stills, awaiting the visitor's intent. Every time I cross its threshold, the woods quietly regards me for some time. When, if, I am finally honest, it enters me.

Self dissolved, senses expanded clean and calm. Clock's tick leaves.

The woods breathes seasons of growth and decay. It smells of time. I believed, sitting there - still believe - that such natural places, and the particular meditation one can enter into through listening to these places, by feeling one with them, can teach us to be at peace with time and with natural cycles.

By sunrise I had been in my tree stand for almost an hour. My body had settled into its comfortable "listen and wait" position. My back was straight against its rest, my right arm on the railing and my right hand held in a fist to keep my fingers warm. My left hand was lightly holding the shotgun between two fingers at the top of its walnut stock. On cold days, holding wood vs. holding metal makes a big difference in finger warmth. The shotgun's weight rested on my seated left thigh, and its barrel on the tree stand's front railing. I clenched and unclenched my toes within my pack boots to keep them warm.

I sat about twenty feet above the ground in the stand, which was located in a wide hedgerow at the border of our farm. The stand had a good view of the fields on either side of the hedgerow, as well as the nearby woods on our neighbor's land. It also had a view of a primary deer path from a large field below, down at the end of the hedgerow. Looking back on either side, along the sides of the large maple tree to which the stand was strapped, I could see up the edges of both fields and into the high grasses of a drainage swale running diagonally on our property. Within fifty yards of the stand was a primary north-south deer trail. This was the catbird seat. I had shot a buck and a doe from this stand on hunting season's opening day.

Sitting for hours in a tree stand is simultaneously an investigation of self and surroundings in a free-association drift. From the stand, I had a 270 degree view, which required me to slightly shift my body from left to right and back again as my gaze traveled the entire range. This was a slow cycle, completed every five minutes or so, and usually it stopped somewhere along its path as I examined something seen or heard: The rustling of dry leaves below by a squirrel, a motion in the woods across the field caught in the corner of my eye, or a mid-distance shotgun blast that could signal deer coming my way.

This action could be a meditation if one was so inclined, and today I was. As in Eastern meditation traditions, the act of hunting placed me firmly in the present, aware of that which my senses usually pass over; the squirrel's rustling akin to the monitoring of my breath. But the oddest sort of duality occurred during this outdoor meditation, as being present in the now was tied to sensing outside myself; in becoming part of my surroundings. Turned around at deeper levels of meditation, the duality became a fusion of self with surroundings. This expansion in my consciousness led me to examine, from a different perspective than is common, my memories and some of my higher questions regarding existence.

One year ago, I began deer hunting again after several years' absence. It was then that I learned this meditation, and I spent almost every morning of the season in the woods. Looking back, what I learned about myself was one of the tipping points that led me to change my life.

Today my meditation centered on the subject of time. In another life time had been my enemy. It was one on a long list of things I thought I could control. I had time for this and not for that, I had time for you and not for her, I could manage time for maximum efficiency. I came to see time like an old fashioned cassette tape recorder, the kind you laid on the table to record a conversation. If I did not like what I was doing, if I was dreading a week at the office, I tried to push the fast forward button on the recorder. I thought I could charge right through the week, and maybe leave some of the tougher tasks for the next week as a consequence. When the weekend or a vacation came, the opposite occurred as I tried to hold the slow button. I counted the hours and days of this, "my" time, making sure all were accounted for: Sunday was the 20% mark of the vacation, Tuesday the 40% mark. What had I accomplished? Had I used every minute responsibly?

This way of thinking about time could also be symbolized by the flow of water. My attempts at the control of time were akin to damming a river to slow its flow, and creating rapids to speed its flow.

When I left the office world, my future stretched out before me as a great, uncharted, steadily flowing river. The dams and rapids of modern life had been removed. For the first time, I had no idea what my future held, nor how to steer towards it. I drifted. Friday held equal weight as Tuesday, 8am the same as

5pm. Eventually I figured out a course, but I resolved never to push and dam time as I had before (except for a few little things, like when I'm waiting for a meal at a restaurant). Releasing this attempt at control brought me peace. I believe this acceptance is a signal that one has found one's true path in life.

As the sun rose higher, I could see more clearly. Yesterday's snow had covered the ground with a half inch of white powder. I could see my pre-dawn tracks coming down from the house, but I saw no deer tracks crossing the shallow part of the drainage swale near my spot, and this was the primary north-south deer trail. I hadn't heard any shots in the stillness either, and had not seen any other hunters. Late in the season as it was, deer rarely moved during the day except when roused by hunters. Certainly I would not rouse any sitting here. But still I sat.

My gaze still moved back and forth around the stand, and the now held me in place. The now holds us all in place; no one can escape the present moment in time. But often our attention is pulled away from the moment we exist in, and I think it leads to much unhappiness and some of our big problems. I had experienced this in several ways.

Often we sacrifice the now for the future. This seems to usually be connected to one's job. "Life is what happens while we are making big plans." I have met many people who endured years of unhappy nows in hope of a better future. Sometimes this was a noble sacrifice, like the Father who worked long hours at a job he was unhappy with to ensure his family's financial security and his childrens' college education, so they could live a more comfortable life than he had. Other times it was a stubborn resolve to pass through years of unhappiness, with the goal of accumulating enough money to take an early retirement. Lastly, and probably most commonly today, it is a weekly sacrifice of Monday through Friday for the future of the weekend, a life lived in weekly packages of quick gratification, living week to week and paycheck to paycheck.

I have also seen people sacrifice the now to cling to the past. This, in particular, alarmed me, like an accelerating train heading toward a concrete wall with no one's hand on the throttle or the brake. The needs of now, today, are changing more quickly than they ever have. Our planet's environment and our impact on it are on a course of accelerating change: natural resource depletion, climate change. I have seen Fundamentalist beliefs hold people to value sets, political systems, and economic systems that once harmonized with our world, but no longer do so. I have watched economics, an inhuman mechanism, dictate what was prudent and what was not regarding the quality of people's lives and the health of the Earth. In particular, I had grown passionate in my old life about the cruel mechanisms tying financial growth and economic well being to the destruction of our environment and to the increasing efficiency required of every worker on their treadmill. Run faster!

Clinging to the past functions as a security net for many. If we don't duplicate what was successful the last time, then what do we do? And how do we know it will work? These questions froze some people into inaction.

I have also seen the most optimistic and proactive leaving of the now: individuals who were willing to make the leap to work within the uncertainty of the future, who recognized that what had worked before may not be appropriate for today or for our future. They boldly stood above the crowd to claim the importance of doing so. These few are creating new structures, systems, and values.

Some months after I left office life, I reconciled my understanding of the importance of now with the need for proactive investigation of the future's needs. My responsibilities on our farm glued me to now. My interaction with nature – walks around the farm, experiencing each day's weather, caring for livestock, working with my hands – required me to be present, and to see the cause and effect of my direct interaction with the natural world. This I approached with a humble attitude; it was my role to carefully observe, just as in my tree stand, the nuances happening around me, and to find the easiest and most synergistic ways to tie my family's livelihood to it.

The now I had tied myself to was infused with my opinion of what was required by the future. I was learning healthy and restorative farming practices. My now was different from those farmers around us who were monocropping GMO's (genetically modified organisms, mainly corn and soybeans), employing practices centered in an outdated model of food production's relationship with the Earth. "Living a different paradigm" is a clichéd way to say this. I had changed my now to live according to how I believed agriculture should function for the future.

Different from my previous life, I found a way to do this that brought me inner peace. I was gently teaching by doing. The proof for any doubter lay in what they could see: the increasing health of the land, its contrast with other destructive farming practices, the money we saved through the simplicity of our practices, our understanding of how to work with nature, and the synergies between the land's health and the health (and taste!) of the livestock we grew.

As to the steadily flowing river, I had no need to struggle against its current. I dropped my oars, and I lost my urgency to pull others along with me, speeding to the future of a drastically changed world. I had decided to live the change, and the life along the shores of the river became healthier as I moved with its current.

Here my thoughts of time ended, sitting in my tree stand with frozen toes. I had reached a point where thoughts of "now" and time intersected with the territory of change and cycle. This was a subject for another time. The day had become sunny, and the new snow made things seem clean and new. There would be no deer moving this morning. I packed up, climbed down, and headed back to warm myself by the woodstove.

Three

It was the mansion dream again.

I called it the mansion because its halls were decorated and it had a warmth of lighting and surface; sconces on the walls and rugs on the floors. Hand painted wallpaper. It was arranged more like a storage building or hotel, with many floors of long straight halls lined by many rooms, too many for me to explore them all. And there did not seem to be a hierarchy to its layout as a large house would have; it was just halls and rooms. There was no entry, no public rooms for visitors. There were no windows, or even a world outside the mansion. But there was a large atrium to which all the halls led, and this seemed more like a warehouse space. On one side of the atrium was a large loading dock. The warehouse seemed foreign to the mansion, like a side of the mansion had been ripped away and the warehouse box attached to it. The torn side of the mansion, with the ends of its halls exposed, reminded me of photos of the torn middle of the Titanic, where it had split in half and its innards had spilled onto the ocean floor.

I also called it the mansion because of the precious objects it held. Room after room along every hall was filled with the most interesting things. They were not in any order - just piled in a giant heap – which filled every room all the way to its high ceiling. Looking into a room was like going to the scrap yard and trying to make out what the objects in the scrap pile had once been. Yes, that was a car, but what's that other thing with a piece sticking out of the pile: a steel truss, part of a farm implement? I never remembered the specific contents of any room; only that they were beautiful, revolutionary, useful, and forgotten.

In this dream - which I had many times over the course of years - I was always in an anxious hurry. My job was to race from door to door down the hall, opening the doors and looking into every room. I did not have time to carefully examine what was in any room, only time to try to remember something that was special about it, and to try to characterize it in my memory so I could describe it to others. The things in each room were so wonderful that I wanted to stay in each to look through its contents! I could not.

Things were chasing me. One by one, they were emptying the rooms with the doors I had opened and carting their contents to the warehouse, where they were boxed and loaded onto trucks at the loading dock. It felt like a chase because I needed to see and remember what was in each room before they caught up with me and emptied it. But they were more like workmen, who did not care about what I was doing; they just had their job to do at their own pace.

There was another entity in the mansion besides the movers and me, a malevolence that really was chasing me. He was in charge of the moving trucks at the loading dock. He never seemed to be near me, I was only aware of his presence somewhere else in the mansion and that he wanted to force me to leave.

I was frantic. There seemed an infinity of rooms and I had to see them all, and at the same time I felt the movers would finish their work soon. Once all the rooms were emptied the mansion would collapse into nothingness, taking me with it.

Early in its iterations, the dream would end there, and I would wake creatively charged with a dim memory of the objects. I wanted to write them down for others to understand, but I could not remember them. I also felt an acute fear for the loss of the mansion. Over the years, the dream expanded to include two final aspects.

I realized I was leaving the doors open for others to see into the rooms, but no one had accompanied me to look inside. I was frustrated that I had defined my job as "the door opener," but no complementary "room investigators" would enter the mansion with me. I did not understand why. There were only the mindless movers and the chasing malevolence.

The second aspect was the little door. One night when I was running down a hall I noticed a little door in the wall at the floor, about two feet tall and one foot wide. It may have been there before although I had never noticed it. It was too small to crawl through, but large enough to kneel down and see through and pass small objects through. It opened with a turn of its knob.

On the other side of the door was blinding sunshine and short cut green grass; a lawn. This extended as far as I could see (which was not far given my eyes' familiarity with the dim mansion's light). I knew this was not a door that led to whatever was outside the mansion, but rather a door to another world. I also knew that whatever I could get through this door would be understood and used by those on the other side (although I never saw them), and would be saved from the movers. The trick, however, was in fitting the objects through the little door.

The dream ended there, and I would wake with a feeling of frustration in knowing there was a place beyond the mansion, through the little door, where the objects in the mansion would not be destroyed and their value would be understood, but that many of the objects were too large to fit through the door. I was caught in a hopeless and lonely conundrum.

During the years I experienced this dream, I woke in the morning and left our home for my job in the city, fifty miles away. I was an architect; principal at a 50 person firm in Syracuse, New York, specializing in educational design; grade schools and colleges. I felt privileged. I had become part owner of the firm at age 31, only nine years out of architecture school. Through a series of role transitions, I had become the leader of the firm's creative development, which was centered around sustainable design; architecture more in harmony with natural systems.

I had the leeway to explore where my mind led me, and the responsibility to bring new ideas from abstraction to implementation on building projects. I set my own hours, chose which projects to become involved with, and never had to worry about my family's financial security. But I was growing more and more anxious, and my dreams were describing the source of my frustrations better than my awake self could. Ironically, my explorations of sustainability had become unsustainable.

*   *   *

Mid December and hunting season was over. The weather had turned consistently cold and snowy; we hadn't had temperatures above freezing for two weeks. We were well prepared for winter. Our freezers were full of chickens, turkeys, and pork for sale, enough to carry us through until the pastured livestock growing season began again in April. Hil had canned or frozen a lot of our garden's produce. I was settling into a daily routine of cracking black walnuts, writing, and taking walks in the woods with a neighbor farmer.

This was the first winter of our family's full-time farming venture, and my first full winter away from office life. I was worried about keeping busy when winter came. But much about the changing seasons felt more natural to me than ever before. Modern life's steady tempo, regardless of weather and season, was in conflict with what our bodies told us: to slow down, change our diet, reduce the radius of our travels to be closer to home and hearth in the cold short days of the northern winter. This worried me, because in previous winters I had tried to avoid these natural urges and felt a need to keep busy.

My daily routine was the key to my harmony with evolution's seasonal clock. Life became quieter. This coincided with a newly-found comfort I had to be more introverted, and to think more about and understand the changes that had taken place within me in the last five years, culminating in my leaving architectural practice.

Almost every day started with cracking walnuts. This was another form of meditation, like the one I had discovered in the tree stand. Engaging one's body in repetitive, simple tasks can free the mind into wandering explorations.

The black walnut trees around our house are giants, some well over 100 years old, and produce thousands of nuts every year. They are slow-growing trees and their lumber is highly valued. Many folks complain about the seasonal messes the trees make when they drop their small green blossoms in the spring, clogging up house gutters, and when they drop their leaves, long leaf stems, and large green-hulled nuts in the fall. Here they are the last tree to leaf in the spring and the first tree to drop leaf in the fall. Every year we spent many hours picking up the nuts and throwing them into the brushy area north of our house.

I love our black walnut trees despite all these things. They are excellent shade trees in the summer, and their branch forms are beautiful in the winter. Plus they give us something for nothing, a food product with no labor to grow: delicious black walnut meat.

Well, not really something for nothing, and that is why black walnut trees are common where we live but black walnut meat is hard to find for sale. Last year we started harvesting the walnuts for their meat, and this year we began selling it. Intense labor, in many steps, is required to liberate the nutmeat from the hulled nut that falls to the ground.

Hilarie, the kids, and I would put the nuts into five gallon buckets as they fell from the trees during September and October. When we had collected ten buckets of nuts (once a week or so), I put them in the gravel driveway in a single layer, and ran over them with the truck, back and forth to crush the hull on every nut. The walnut that fell from the tree has two parts: the soft green hull, usually about an inch thick, and the woody nut in the middle of the hull. After I had driven over them I could pick the nut out of the crushed hull.

The first time I did this last year, I did not wear gloves, and my hands were stained black for more than a month, until the stained layers of skin wore off. Walnut hulls make a powerful brown/black dye, and could be boiled to make ink and clothing dye. Now I wear gloves!

Once the nuts were picked out of their hulls and collected back into five gallon buckets (a kneeling back-straining task that took an hour or more), they were placed into an old cement mixer for washing. This washing was necessary to remove any hull residue that remained, as it would sour the meat if left on. I dumped one bucket in and turned on the mixer while spraying in water with a garden hose. When the water turned black and thick with hull remnants I turned off the mixer and held a piece of plywood partially over its opening, leaving a small gap at the bottom while tilting the mixer to dump the dirty water. This needed to be repeated a half dozen times until the water came out clear.

Next the washed walnuts were dumped from the mixer back into the bucket, then onto a chicken-wire bottomed three foot by three foot drying rack. The rack was left to dry outside for the rest of the day, then placed into the "rack stack," a fifteen rack vertical storage unit I had built that was kept in the workshop. The walnuts would cure here for three weeks minimum, in which time the meat would change from soft, tasteless, and white to crunchy, smoky and rich, with a much denser flavor than the English walnuts available in the grocery store.

The black walnut is distinguished from the English walnut by its flavor, and also by its shell. The English walnut has a thin shell that can be cracked with a small hand nutcracker, and the black walnut has a thick, tremendously strong shell most commonly cracked in a shop vise or with a hammer on concrete. The difficulty of cracking the shell, and the accompanying difficulty of cracking the shell without also smashing the meat into little bits, is the reason black walnut meat is rarely sold in this area.

I had found an ace-in-the-hole to deal with this issue: a company in Iowa that made a motorized black walnut cracking machine. I had seen an online video of the machine at work, and true to the manufacturer's claims, it cleanly cracked the shells with the meat falling out in "fancy" grade whole quarters. I ordered the machine and it arrived just as the first rounds of nuts had cured. The machine only cracked one nut at a time. A nut was placed in a holder and a vertical steel shaft connected to the motor by a cam slowly cracked the nut. I could crack about 100 nuts per hour. Not speedy but significantly faster and neater than the hammer!

By the beginning of November we had racked about 9,000 nuts. I had sold about twenty quarter pound bags at farmers markets by that time, for about $1.00 per ounce, and demand seemed good. So I resolved to spend the beginning of each winter day by cracking at least 60 nuts. When enough accumulated in the refrigerator we vacuum packed and froze them, to be thawed, roasted, bagged, and sold at next year's markets.

I knew I'd never become rich selling black walnuts. The machine had cost $450 and I'd be lucky to make the money back in the first year. Oftentimes we do things for reasons other than their economics. The availability of walnuts was an alignment to me; something nature was providing I felt some obligation to make use of. It seemed thrifty to not throw them away, and noble to teach others about a little-known food. Besides, the nuts had to be picked up anyway. And the time spent cracking them during the winter was "cheap time," when there were few other tasks needing to be done.

Every day after breakfast, I spent an hour or so

alone in the workshop, cracking black walnuts. While I cracked the walnuts, I thought. I meditated. I drifted. I spent time working on the giant puzzle I had been working on all my life and most intensely the past five years, the same I think all of us work on: what is life's meaning and our place in the universe? The nature of time was one part of that puzzle, most recently visited in my tree stand. But there were many other topics I had been working on.

Today I thought about my old recurring dream of the mansion, which had disappeared for a while after I left the office world. The mansion represented the puzzle; my search for answers and the urgency of it, the difficulty of relaying what I had learned to others and trying to teach them how to implement it in architectural practice, and how alone and sometimes abandoned I had felt.

Thinking along this path, I remembered the dream had resurfaced several months after I left work, while I was still trying to find the way for the next part of my life. It all made sense to me now.

*   *   *

I had been absent from the mansion for a long time. I walked to it from the outside. It actually had a place; land around it overgrown with hedges, trees, and vines. I had the feeling all this had grown up since my last visit to the interior, although I had never suspected there was an outside to the building. The movers were gone, the malevolence was gone; this felt like my own home, though much larger. There was no evidence of the warehouse or loading dock.

The jungle of plants around the structure did not allow me to understand the size and shape of the building. There was a walk that led through the overgrowth to a front door, a door I had never seen from the inside before.

There was a new presence with me: the realtor, who was to give me a tour of the mansion. She unlocked the front door, which led to an enclosed porch wrapping two sides of the mansion. We had to walk the length of the porch to get to the door that led into the house. The porch was lined with windows to the outside, and these admitted green sunlight filtered through vines hanging in front of the windows. The porch was lined with crates, pots, gardening tools, bicycles, and many other things you would find in a garage or garden shed. Between all these things was an aisle; a long path from front door to inner door.

The realtor unlocked the inner door and we walked inside. I trusted her to keep me safe, the two of us seemed a small spark of light in this immense dark structure. She would not allow me to get lost as I had before. She told me to look only in the front rooms of the house, that these were where a house lived. I did not want to go upstairs anyway.

The front rooms were comfortable, with a nice flow from one to another. There were fresh perspectives of the other rooms, depending on my vantage point; which room I was standing in. The realtor was beside me all this time.

And the things inside the rooms! An eclectic

collection of objects. I could be still and examine their intricacies and their relationships to one another. I could imagine myself sitting in one of the rooms' comfortable armchairs for hours, gazing at the meaningful things contained within.

Now I was above the mansion and could see through its walls. The front rooms glowed within a flashlight's circle, while halls and rooms in the stories above remained dark. I saw myself sitting alone in the parlor staring; I will live here a while.

What lay here, within my reach , that in this smaller place I could touch, watch, day after day, was different than the abstractions of my wanderings in the upper stories.

I could not say which was more important. I knew they both had their place: my resting observation of touchable nuance and my exploration of limitless possibility. I knew I was meant to cross the thresholds of the upper stories' rooms again someday, when I had the wisdom to peacefully examine their contents.

Four

It's funny, but I don't remember much about my last day as an architect. Maybe that was because I didn't know it was my last day. My partners had agreed to my proposal to take a six month leave of absence, and I assumed I would be back to work after that.

I remember the date of my departure: February seventh. This date and its semi-annual partner, August seventh, would come to hold particular significance in the future. It had been announced to the staff that I was temporarily leaving. I packed up my desk, taking only the things I thought I might need during the six months, but leaving a substantial amount of my stuff at the desk. The desk would remain unoccupied during my leave, and I would be able to access my company email and the company's file server from my laptop at home via the PC on the office desk.

I wrote an email saying goodbye to everyone at the firm, and how much I would miss them. I said personal goodbyes to those I cared for most. And that is all I remember about that day.

Things had been building toward that last day for a year. In January of the year before, I took a day trip to one of my partner's homes to do some strategic planning centered around a website I had been using to share my writing about architectural design. I rode to her house with another one of my partners. During our conversation, I realized for the first time how little of the work I had done was understood by my partners.

My partners had always been extremely supportive of me and the creative direction in which I was leading the firm. We had made good progress in the past four years under that direction, and we were stretching our design work into exciting new territory. But my leadership into that territory was focusing more and more on philosophical abstraction. I asserted that responsible, sustainable design and the industry change required therein was less about tangible things (reducing energy consumption, changing manufacturing processes, understanding how to build to maximize the benefits of the local climate via passive solar design, on and on) and more about emotion, understanding the psychology of change, and what motivates people through the hardship of change.

I also strongly felt that it was architecture's role to express new, healthier relationships between humankind and nature, between humans themselves, and that buildings could do this through the materials we used to construct them and how those materials aged. Architects needed to learn how to sense the energies of the places in which we built, and to learn to build in harmony with them. Not only literal energies such as sunlight and those embodied in the materials we used, but also the energies people and communities invested in places; how much they cared for them and the memories each place held. All together, this resulted in my focusing on understanding, treasuring and caring for what we have as the path to a sustainable future. This was away from the direction most of the sustainable design industry was moving, with its focus on measurable building performance criteria, and harder for others to understand, including my partners.

In the year following the January meeting, leading up to my departure thirteen months later, my feelings of separation from my partners grew. They were still very supportive, but I felt I had disabled their personal growth by leading them someplace where they could only follow and not creatively contribute. I knew the work I was doing was important, but I felt alone and grew increasingly depressed.

I did have a support group in the firm: about ten individuals my partners and I had recognized as being able to contribute to the philosophy I was developing. We decided to staff our most forward-leaning projects, the ones with the most potential, with members of this group, and the group met regularly to discuss our direction. We started working on a book, the concepts of which were prominently arranged on the main conference room wall. We also started work on a new school project, the largest our firm had ever undertaken and filled with exciting new ways we were implementing our philosophy. I was very proud of these people, and happiest at our meetings and the public presentations we did. New concepts were flowing out of me on a weekly basis, straight into project environments. I had never been more productive.

Even with all this support my depression grew. I was sensitive to the negative energy coming back to me from the other members of the firm who were not involved in these projects. I had become tired from my years of pulling the firm toward deep change; it had gradually worn me out. I keenly felt the loss of the kinship of my partners, who I had grown with over the past twenty years, building our firm from ten to as many as seventy-five people.

Most of all, I held a deep sense that I was on the wrong path. I knew I was in pursuit of the right things regarding the changes needed in today's world, but the vehicle of architecture was a poor and indirect way for me to participate in making those changes happen. At my worst times, I felt the whole thing, my whole architectural philosophy, was an overly-complicated sham.

After I returned from a long Christmas and New Years vacation, I proposed the details of a leave of absence to my partners, starting in February after my immediate project obligations had been met.

I was exhausted. I had spent four years as the principle change agent within the firm, and I had learned a lot about the nature of change, mostly from my failed attempts to change others. My early methods seem so naïve to me now!

The earliest strategy implemented, which is still heavily used in sustainable and environmental design, but translatable to any endeavor (as all the methods I will outline are), is the "stick and carrot." I never cared much for this method, even in the beginning, because it treated people as Pavlovian simpletons. First whack them with the stick: scare them with doomsday scenarios about the end of the world if we stay on our present course, or penalize them financially, as our government often does with those violating environmental regulations. Next show them the carrot, which could be a financial incentive for doing the right thing, a bonus or promotion at work, time off, etc.

Instead, I modeled change for others at our firm. This focused on the end benefits of changing to do the right thing. These benefits could be a better world, a healthier community and environment, a more successful firm, and the pride in accomplishing something new. It focused on the positive and was Pollyanna-ish regarding the negative: change is hard. Change is hard in a business environment because efficiency is lost when established processes are changed, and new time needs to be taken to figure out new ways of doing things. And change is hard because with change comes risk, risk that the new process or widget you are using won't work correctly in the field, risk that the lawyers will come after you when something in the building you designed fails and you have no track record of similar products' performance or best practice to fall back upon.

Despite my strategy, the stick and carrot was still in the background: those that followed the firm's direction would be rewarded, and those that didn't would be penalized. This always bothered me; I could never understand why people couldn't see the sense of my arguments and agree to follow via their own motivation.

My partners were of the opinion we should stay the course, keep reinforcing to the staff the direction we had chosen, and keep producing projects that showed the validity of that direction via their success. I still felt negative energy coming back at me from some members of the firm. Sometimes this was overt, and these folks were eventually let go as incompatible with our firm's culture. Again, I felt partially responsible.

I was the guy with the new ideas who at the same time was ill-equipped psychologically to deal with the implications of implementing the change these new ideas necessitated. And, it was a constant struggle. I would often talk to my partners about "what the firm wanted to be" if left to its own devices; what would happen if I stopped pulling on it to change. Changing the firm in the manner I was using was like trying to move a boulder half buried in the earth with a giant rubber band. If I pulled hard enough I could unseat the boulder and half-pull it out of its hole. But the second I let go, the boulder would fall back to its seated position.

After years of agonizing over this, I came to understand the true nature of change. Change is based in emotion. People can only deeply change from the inside; they can only change themselves, and change originates in the heart before the head. I may be able to show them a bright and new path, but only they contain the motivation to take the first steps down that path; only they can decide if the hardship involved in change is worth the end result. And sadly, realistically, most people are too afraid to take that first step toward change, which really is a giant leap. I also found that in general (but not always), the older the individual, the harder it was for them to change.

I had taken on an impossible responsibility to change the firm. I really could only work with those who were inclined to take their leap. Toward the end of my career in architecture I had realized this, and the folks who formed the group within the firm with whom I most worked were the ones able to take that first leap.

On February seventh, I left the firm feeling spent, empty. I did not know what I would do for the next six months. I was in pain dwelling on the psychological afterimages of my experiences.

I don't remember very much about my first month away. It was winter so I fell back on my usual wintertime woodworking projects, but my heart wasn't in them anymore. I went to see a lot of matinees. I felt like a retired person, out in the middle of the day when the roads were empty and most people my age were at work. Hilarie was home with Henry during this time, and her support helped me through this difficult period. She was always there to listen, and never grew tired of doing so, even though the things I needed to talk to her about, the things I was working through inside, were dismal.

Hilarie and I had met in the fall of 1993. I had remained in Syracuse after receiving a bachelor of architecture degree at Syracuse University in 1991. When I graduated, the economy was in a slump and few architectural firms were hiring. I took a job mowing commercial properties, plowing snow, and driving a street sweeping truck at night.

By March, 1993 the economy had improved, and I went to work for a small architectural firm in Syracuse. I'll never forget my first day: the blizzard of '93 had deposited 50 inches of snow on the city over the three previous days, and I had worked day and night all weekend plowing. I went in for my first day on Monday with only a few hours of sleep. This was the firm I would stay at for the next twenty years.

In the fall of 1993 I was living on the east side of Syracuse with two roommates: Anne and Alyce. Anne was an architect at another firm downtown that specialized in historic renovation. Alyce was a registered nurse in the intensive care unit at Community General Hospital on the south side of Syracuse. For about a month, Alyce kept pressuring me to meet a friend who worked with her. Finally, in October, I met Alyce's friend, Hilarie at a downtown pub named Mulrooney's.

Hilarie had grown up downstate, in Wappingers Falls near the Hudson River. Her mother worked at IBM, and her Father was a teacher. They had divorced when she was four years old, and she had lived with her mother, stepfather, sister, two stepsisters, and stepbrother. She had received her associate degree in nursing at Dutchess Community College, then attended the State University of New York Health Science Center in Syracuse, where she received her bachelor of science in nursing in spring, 1993. The first time I met Hil at Mully's, I was struck by her beautiful smile, and strangely enough, by how cagey she seemed. It turned out we enjoyed many of the same things; science fiction, metal rock music, and quiet time at home.

We were married two years later. The year after, in 1996, we moved from Syracuse back to my family's farm. Starting in 2002, we had three children.

Throughout the 20 years I had known her, Hil supported me in everything, starting with our big leap to renovate the decrepit old farmhouse with little prior construction experience. She always believed in me, and we always helped each other through rough times. This was probably the worst time, and she was there; assured me she would always be there.

I was rapidly changing inside. This was automatic, beyond my control. Some examples: I had been reading everything I could get my hands on regarding environmentalism, the nature of change, etc., for years. Now I quit reading entirely. I could not watch the news and I could not listen to the radio, they upset me too much. I didn't care about what the rest of the world seemed to care about, and was especially infuriated by the way pop-culture had taken over the morning news. Hilarie learned to turn off the TV when I came downstairs in the morning. Soon we quit watching TV almost entirely; I felt its programs and advertisements were telling me who I should be and how I should live, and its messages were shallow and false. Most worrisome to me was that I quit writing. Writing had been my primary creative outlet. I had written an essay a week for years; it was my best vehicle for exploring my mind and finding new ideas. Now that connection was gone. I felt a friend had left.

New things began to fill the voids left by the removal of the old. I wanted to listen to music. I loved roots music, bluegrass, and the blues. I loved the rich local music scene. I began playing my acoustic guitar after a twenty year hiatus; this replaced the television in the evenings. I lost my self-consciousness; I started growing my hair and my beard, and didn't care what others thought of my appearance. I spent long periods doing nothing while my thoughts slowly simmered. I could never do this under my old "dam and rapid" control of time.

My dreams still let me know of my subconscious' activities. The mansion was gone, at least for now. Other disturbing dreams replaced it; this empty period right after leaving work contained more dreams than I had ever experienced. I remember the dreams were disturbing but I do not remember much of their specific content. They were never violent; it was a disjointedness that made them disturbing, they were about confusion. There is only one dream I remember in detail, which spoke perfectly of my situation.

*   *   *

The overloaded ferry was approaching the terminal. It was top-heavy, loaded with people on its upper decks. Each deck was organized with a large room down the middle of the boat, packed to standing room only. On either side of the large room, running the length of the boat's exterior, were narrow corridors. Two people could not pass each other in the corridors without turning sideways. The corridors had narrow and steep stairways at their ends, and one had to duck to miss hitting the bulkhead while climbing the stairs. The stairs were so narrow that two people could not pass each other on them; one had to back up to the top or bottom of the stair's single run to let the other through. The ferry's interior had no windows to the outside.

Someone announced the ferry was near the terminal, and those wishing to depart must leave quickly, because the ferry would not be there for long. The perimeter corridors and the narrow stairs were the only way down to disembark, and everyone started pushing toward the doorways that led to the corridors. I was near the middle of the room and stuck in the crowd.

Suddenly, person-sized square holes started appearing in the floor, and people started falling into them. I stood in one place and watched the checkerboard of holes develop. Frightened people ran for the corridor doorways and fell into the holes. I didn't know where they fell to, but it was not to the deck below; it seemed they just disappeared. Still I stood in one place, and eventually, new holes stopped

49

appearing. I walked around the holes to the crowded corridor.

People were pushing against each other in the corridor, trying to make it past each other to one stair or the other at the corridor ends. I pushed and slid between others until I was at the stairs, then I barreled down the stairs with such momentum, almost falling down the stairs' steepness, that others moving upward were forced back down.

I appeared inside the terminal. The terminal was like a shopping mall, it had two levels with escalators, stores, and restaurants. It had two ends. One was a vacant cul-de-sac with an escalator occupying part of it, and it always had a few people standing around in its emptiness. The other was a wide window and door-filled wall with a many-laned highway running parallel and just outside it. Vehicles zoomed by in both directions, but none stopped at the terminal.

I recognized a lot of people in the terminal (in various iterations of this dream I would have conversations with specific people I knew in real life, but I could not remember the topics discussed). The terminal had no place for its occupants to rest. No surface was level, and every floor and wall was at an odd angle, even in the restaurants where many of my conversations occurred. The best repose I could find was by standing and leaning against a steeply sloping wall.

At many places around the terminal there were screens listing arrivals and departures, and periodically announcements were made, but I could not read the language on the screens or understand the announcements. I did not know what to do. Sometimes I would wait and wait, and eventually the dream would end. Other times I would leave the terminal and start walking along the highway, which was raised above the ground like an overpass, but I had no idea where it led and I never got very far.

*   *   *

I had time to kill while I waited for direction, and waited for the painful afterimages of my work at the firm to fade. I had some confidence I would eventually know my way again, it would just take time.

So, I started buying time. Literally. There was a regular Friday evening antiques auction in a neighboring town, and I began attending. I enjoyed watching the regulars that came to the auction every week, filling the old yellow vinyl-covered theater chairs in the rundown auction house, which stank of years' worth of tobacco smoke and burnt hamburgers. It was a sort of Friday night social club; a place to eat bad food and look for deals.

I usually arrived there an hour early and parked in the frozen rutted lot in the darkness. I carried the sandwich dinner Hilarie had made and walked past the people smoking outside the door and into the concrete block building. I stopped just inside to give the attendant my last name, and she gave me a card with a number on it that I would hold up if I wanted to bid on something. I went to the seating area and claimed my chair by leaving my coat, dinner and card on it. I spent the rest of the time before the auction started browsing the items for sale.

The auctioneer always started promptly at 6:00. He didn't care if the crowd kept talking, social club that it was. He had a crew of a half dozen men carrying objects to be bid on to the front of the room and holding them up, one by one in a revolving train. The auctioneer always started high and worked down until he received his first bid, "50 dollars here – 40 – tweeenty-fiiiive dollars. Don't be so cheap now." Eventually he would get a hit from a bidder, and back up he went until the bidders would go no higher. Sometimes he'd whine about the steal the highest bidder had just gotten. It was all a game.

Every Friday the house's tables and walls were packed with paintings, lamps, china and carnival glass, flatware, old postcards, pocket watches, furniture, and clocks. Things were sold in a specific order. The first hour was all crap to be unloaded - $1 to $30 things. The good stuff came in the next few hours – antique desks, tables, chairs, old coins; almost any household object you can think of - and clocks. The auctioneer specialized in old clocks. Some evenings he would auction off as many as forty clocks, drawing bidders all the way from Rochester to Pennsylvania.

At 9 or 10:00 the whole thing would fall apart. Most of the good stuff would be gone, and the crowd would be half what it had started at. If I had the fortitude, this was when the real deals could be had. The auctioneer would tell the remaining bidders to bring anything they were interested in up to an empty table in the front, and he would sell everything on the table before shutting down for the night. Usually only one or two people were interested in any given thing on the table, so things went cheap. At the end of the night there always was a lot of stuff left unsold. Some of it would reappear at the following week's auction, but most of it went someplace else; I have no idea where.

Most weeks I came home with an old clock or two. I preferred the kind with a swinging pendulum, and powered by either weights or coil springs. I learned how to repair them by examining their gears (a clock's gears and all its other timekeeping parts are collectively called its movement), and looking for clues as to what had stopped their tick. Ninety percent of the time something simple had stopped the clock. Its beat may need adjustment; the swing of the pendulum was adjusted by slightly bending the crutch wire to one side or the other to create an evenly spaced "tick-tock-tick-tock" rhythm. The crutch wire had a loop on the end of it that wrapped around the pendulum's rod and gave it a slight push on every swing, keeping the clock on a steady beat. Or a piece had broken that I could make; a lantern gear missing a spoke, or a coil spring missing the wire which held its ratchet gear dog in place, holding the spring wound.

During the first months of my leave I loved repairing clocks. The ones with no obvious broken parts always suffered from a clock's worst enemy: friction. Friction was caused by corrosion, old hardened clock oil, grime, and worn parts. I have yet to buy a clock (and I have over thirty now), that could not be made to run again by reducing friction through disassembly and a thorough cleaning.

First I would remove the movement from the clock's case and photograph all six sides of it, in case I ran into problems remembering what went where during its reassembly. Then I would put all the parts into a bath of denatured alcohol and let them soak for a day or two. Movements are made of brass and steel, and the alcohol softened grime on the parts without leaving an oily residue which would attract dust after the movement was reassembled.

A clock's movement is a simple mechanical device. It has two brass plates held together with brass pillar posts. Each plate has holes in it (called pivots) within which the gears' axles rotate. The plates hold the clock's gears in place.

Old clocks typically have two trains. A train is a series of gears that turn one after another, usually four to six in a train. The right train keeps time, and the left train controls the clock's hourly chime. Energy is stored either in a hanging weight or a wound spring, and it travels through the time train to the clock's escapement, which is the tick-tock gear powering the crutch wire via the verge, a "U" shaped piece of steel that only allows the escapement gear to rotate one tooth at a time. Energy in the chime train moves through the gears and escapes via the chime hammer, which is tripped by pegs on a large counting wheel to strike the chime.

Once the parts had been soaked, I picked them out of the alcohol one by one and cleaned the dirt off them with an old toothbrush. Special attention was required at certain areas. Each pivot in the clock's two plates was cleaned by working a toothpick around and around in the hole, capturing the sticky old clock oil clinging inside it. Each brass gear had a steel axle, the ends of which fit into the pivot holes in the plates. Often these axles were grooved from years' worth of dirt working around in the pivot, and sometimes they were also corroded. The fit and cleanliness of the axle end in the pivot was the number one source of friction. I looked at the axle's ends through a magnifying glass and polished them with fine emery cloth until they were smooth and bright. There were other steps to cleaning: straightening coil springs and rubbing off old hardened grease, cleaning lantern gears with the toothbrush until their spokes turned freely, etc. But the pivots and axle ends were the major concern.

Once all the parts were clean, I laid them on a paper towel arranged by train: chime and time. Then I reinserted the axles into the bottom plate's pivots one by one, starting with the mainspring or weight winding spool, proceeding through to the escapement or the counting wheel, depending on the train. Now came the most difficult part: setting the top plate on the assembly and aligning all the axles into the top plate's holes. Sometimes this took 5 minutes, sometimes an hour. It was a process of reaching into the movement and pushing the axle of each gear to align with the hole in the top plate, without unseating the axles I had already positioned. The most rewarding part of the whole process was the final click I heard as the last axle fell into place and the top plate dropped fully into position.

The rest (hopefully) was simple. I applied a small

drop of oil to the little well around each pivot in both plates, the hole within which the gears' axles rotated. Then the movement was reinserted into the case, the beat adjusted, and the clock left in the workshop for a week or so to make sure all was working correctly.

Many times the movement had to be disassembled and reassembled several times after cleaning, as I troubleshot some problem in the meshing of the gears. Sometimes the pivot holes in the plates would need to be rebushed (drilled out and a new round brass bushing set in the hole) so the axle rotated with less slop within the pivot and its gear's teeth meshed better with its neighbors.

Clock repair is a vocation of patience and detail. It was yet another form of meditation. It occupied much of my time moving through a period of uncertainty following my February departure from work.

I was keeping in regular contact with an old high school friend at the time. She insightfully noticed how appropriate it was I had taken up clock repair during a period in which I was coming to grips with a new relationship with time, away from that of the office world. The gears of my subconscious were working even as I patiently cleaned the gears of the old clocks in my workshop.

Five

It was early July and our one small chest freezer was full of chickens. Many more were growing in the pasture. Until this time we had sold to friends all the chicken we produced. Now our production had increased to the point where we needed a larger customer base. Hilarie and I were brainstorming ways to market our products. Chicken was just the beginning. We had turkeys and pigs on the pasture to sell in the fall, and an expanded flock of seventy laying hens who would eventually be producing about thirty dozen eggs per week.

We had named our farm "Just a Few Acres," the same name it held as my parents' beef farm when I was a kid. I had set up a farm website and Facebook page in April. They had gained a few followers but they were people we already knew. I created a farm pamphlet and had two hundred printed. We posted copies on the bulletin boards at the town ice cream stand, supermarket, and YMCA. Still no calls.

I visited Keith Thomson, a farmer who lived down the hill from us on our road. Keith had a vegetable CSA (community supported agriculture). I had been acquainted with his wife, Sarah, way back when I was in high school and we both worked at a local plant nursery. I never knew her very well, and I had never met Keith, who was a retired junior high school science teacher. Keith gave me a tour of his farm. He grew his produce in a collection of hoop houses and outdoor gardens, and he served about forty families with weekly shares of produce.

When I asked Keith about how he marketed, the answer was mostly through word-of-mouth. He had gradually grown his CSA over the last ten years and it was now slightly larger than the size he wanted to stabilize at; he had more than enough work. He had a reputation as a meticulous farmer with excellent quality produce and loyal share holders. He struck me as a thoughtful and kind person. We were to become fast friends.

Keith sold his surplus produce at a farmers market held every Friday morning in the parking lot of the Triphammer Marketplace, a mall about fifteen minutes away from where we lived. He recommended I visit the market, and that I may want to start vending there. At least I could talk to the other vendors to learn more about how they got the word out about what they were growing.

Friday morning I drove into the parking lot where the farmers market was held. It was sunny and hot, especially on the pavement. The vendors stood under their individual tents talking with each other and a few customers. The main draw at the market was the fish truck. It had been coming to the mall parking lot every Friday morning for the last thirty years and had a loyal following. There was always a line of people waiting to buy fresh seafood sold from the back door of the refrigerated truck. A few years ago, the mall's owners had graciously allowed other vendors to set up at no charge when the fish truck was there.

The market was arranged behind the truck, with vendors' tents on both sides of the fish truck's waiting line. There were about fifteen vendors outside selling produce, maple syrup, baked goods, meats (but no chicken!) and honey. There were more vendors inside the mall atrium selling crafts: jewelry, clothing, soap, paintings, etc.

I walked to Keith's tent and he introduced me to his neighbors on either side: Eileen Scheffler, who had an organic dairy and beef farm just up the hill from our farm (another neighbor I sadly had never met), and Pat Tinker, the egg lady. I received more questions than I asked that day, mostly from the egg lady, "What's your business plan, how large do you want to grow, how is your product different, what's your marketing strategy?" I didn't have very good answers. My head was spinning.

This seemed a good market to start out at. It was low-key, the vendors seemed like nice people and were friendly to each other, no one else was selling chicken, and it was free! I left the market with the phone number of the mall manager. By the end of the day I had been approved to vend the next Friday.

I imagined lines at our tent like at the fish truck. Friends who had tried our chicken said it was very good; it just was a matter of getting more people to take a first taste to get them hooked. There were so many details to take care of! We had to buy a standard ten foot by ten foot market tent. We needed a table, chairs, a sign identifying our farm and products, some large coolers, a cash box, calculator, receipt pad...I had everything together by the next Monday, and set it up in the driveway to make sure I hadn't missed anything. It was sparse compared to the displays of the produce vendors, but it would do for now.

The next Friday I arrived at the parking lot at 7:00am and was set up by 7:15. The fish truck had been there since before 7:00 but the hours for the other vendors were formally 8:00 to noon. There was one other vendor setting up. The fish truck was doing a brisk business already. I sat down in my folding chair, cooled myself off, and waited.

Soon other vendors arrived and started setting up. Keith, Eileen, and Pat the egg lady showed up and set up in spots adjacent to mine. I learned that tent placement was a touchy thing at farmers markets; you set up where you were assigned and nowhere else. Vendors jockeyed for the most prominent spots from season to season. I said my hellos, helped my neighbors with their tents, and sat back down. I waited and watched.

There was a good vibe here. I later learned it was not unique to this market. Since then, every market I've attended has had a peace and positivity about it. The vendors, although they may be selling the same products, are friendly and cooperative with each other. We're all pulling in the same direction, trying to connect consumers more directly to their food supply and educate them about the positive health, environmental, and economic benefits of eating local. The customers linger to talk to the vendors, in stark contrast to the faceless "grab and go" feel of a supermarket.

And both the vendors and the customers have such interesting stories to tell! Many of the vendors, like me, had lives before farming. The soap lady was a teacher in New Jersey. Keith was a science teacher in our town. The young man that sells produce grown using draft animals was an English major in college. The woman selling granola is also a Baptist pastor. This market was the beginning of my belonging to a community of local farmers who often cared for one another almost as family.

As I got to know them, I learned many of our customers also had diverse and interesting backgrounds. These bonds were important to us. We wanted to form a community with our customers, not only because they were paying us for our products, but also because we felt pride in helping to feed their families, proud of the direct connection we had made from our land to their table.

A woman named Marcia bought one of our chickens the very first day we attended the market. She came back the next week raving about our chicken, it was the best she'd ever had (I was thinking to myself: speak louder Marcia!). Since that day she has purchased one chicken every week. During the winter we deliver a month's supply, four chickens, to her house when we are out running other errands, and always stay twenty minutes to chat. Marcia had also lived two lives: she was an archeologist who had worked in the Middle East, and now telecommuted to work for a London, UK company. Her husband wrote ancient history books, five of which had been published and a sixth in the middle of a deal for Hollywood movie rights.

Keith and Eileen helped me a lot in those early days at the market. Keith advertised our chicken to his CSA members, and always reported how good it was to someone who was on the fence about buying one at the market. Eileen had a quiet, knowing, positivity about her. She cared about how everyone else was doing, spent time at every market checking in with the other vendors, listened carefully to what they said and sometimes offered gentle advice, and never had anything negative to say about anyone else. She and her husband Ed had raised three kids on their farm, which was small by today's dairy standards, by being smart and thrifty. I thought of her as a role model for how to treat others at the market.

That first day I sold six chickens, taking in $102. I was happy despite my naïve dreams of a line of customers to my tent. I had been introduced to a community of like-minded people, whose connections would grow throughout the rest of the season into a larger community than I had ever felt a member of before. I learned that for most vendors, farmers markets were not the principle way they sold their products. Instead, they were the primary marketing method for adding regular customers to their sales list. I also learned that consistency was key: show up every week and stay the duration of the market so your customers could count on you being there.

The customer/ farming community that populated the farmers markets was a stark contrast to the old business community I had been a member of in my previous life. At the market, there was often a noble feeling of helping others for help's sake alone. The modern world, for whatever reasons, seems to be pushing us away from this attitude. Maybe this is part of the glue that has been lost as communities disintegrate. Community members used to help each other without a balance sheet, without an expectation of something in return. I had seen this in my father's contributions to our community, and I felt called to act in the same spirit with my new found farming community.

When I was an architect, I had begun to understand the importance of this karmic attitude toward working for the health of the whole, felt the world was degenerating into an accounting view of social life, and it was damaging communities. I named this attitude Transactionalism: Life considered as a series of deposits and withdrawals. You scratch my back and I'll scratch yours.

The more I looked, the more undercurrents of transactionalism I found. In biology, there was a concept called "reciprocal altruism," a behavior whereby an organism acted in a manner that temporarily reduced its fitness while increasing another organism's fitness, with the expectation that the other organism would act in a similar manner at a later time.

I tolerated some of this in business, and absolutely cringed at it in personal life. In business it could be mostly harmless, a simple form of cooperation, as in "hey buddy from the business next door, I have a client that I could hook you up with, if you'll help me get that other client I've been chasing..." And it could range to truly distasteful backstabbing and ladder climbing; á la some '80's Wall Street clichés. There was a temptation to see people as transactional devices. This could lead to different moral sets in different settings, a chameleon nature, as we tried to get what we wanted out of others. It seemed this attitude was increasingly leaking out of the business environment, and into friendships and community life.

Transactionalism was life oversimplified; everything in pluses and minuses, deposits and withdrawals. And when poorly practiced it was so transparent as to make one feel used, commoditized, and expended for transactional worth.

I felt, knew, a beautiful way of seeing beyond transactionalism. Life's real deposits and withdrawals were a vastly complex flow of interrelated wholes. Most simply, a whole could be a person, but it could also be a farmers market, a business, or a community. You and me, our relationship over time, a community's health, was one example of flowing, weaving, interrelated wholes. You could keep a ledger of that relationship, but see the nuance that would be lost? The modern world had lost that knowledge; too much had become black and white, one pole or another, plus or minus. An altruistic richness had been lost.

Together, we all make a great river. Think of our relationships over time. We affect each others' courses in complex ways, and no accountant can keep a balance. The flow has causal links, but their complexity is unmappable.

When we see this way; that of a great river; it becomes a morality: goodness to others for the sake of that goodness alone. Those of us with religion know this and sometimes we forget its true meaning: goodness as positive energy to the collective flow, and not as a transactional relationship with God. The idea of St. Peter at the gates with a ledger, although simple to understand, sells God short. Prayer as a form of bargaining does the same.

But I never wanted this view to be argued only from spirituality or religion, I wanted it to be about our health, broadly embraceable by those with diverse viewpoints. So I came up with one big assertion and a widely applicable example.

Assertion: The most fulfilling relationships are those where the individual contributes to the health of the noble system without regard to the net flow of their transactions, and where the individual has tied their health to the health of the noble system. You could replace "fulfilling" with "meaningful," "healthy," "moral," or "sustainable," depending on your lens. "Noble" intends a system with good purpose. And system is any collection of more than one, all the way up to the universe.

Example: Family. Each member of a healthy family system contributes positive actions into the system with the health of the family foremost in mind, and with no ledger balance to be settled. The health of the family member is dependent on the health of the family. The purpose of the family is noble, most clearly felt when there are children. This is love. The farmers market community often functioned as a family in this way.

Within a few weeks I was selling at two markets: the first at Triphammer on Fridays, and another in Homer, about a half hour away, on Saturdays. The Homer market was held in a beautiful park on Main Street. Like at Triphammer, the Homer market started with me meeting some interesting characters. I was also able to put my beliefs of a "great river" goodness to others in practice, through helping a person in need.

My involvement with the Homer market started one Saturday when I stopped there to meet the vendors and get a feel whether it would be an appropriate place to vend. Quickly I learned no one else was selling chicken. Some of the Homer vendors also sold at the Triphammer market, but many did not. The Homer market was organized by a volunteer Board with a President and subcommittees focused on various things: membership, advertising, fundraising, etc. There was a lot of work that needed to be done behind the scenes to create a successful market. Vendors directed me to the market manager, Tina, who was employed by the Board to oversee market logistics. She informed me that my first step in joining this market was to submit an application to the membership committee. I took an application, sat on a park bench to fill it out, and gave it to a vendor who was also part of the membership committee.

When I met Tina, the market manager, she asked me if I did my own butchering Yes, I did. As I was filling out my membership application, Anna Dallam, a livestock farmer who sold pork at the market, approached me, introduced herself, and asked if I had a motorized chicken plucker. Yes, I did. She asked if I would be interested in helping out a disabled Vietnam vet who had 100 meat chickens ready for butchering. Yes, I was. I was keen to form as many new connections as I could, and this was a way to meet some new folks while doing a good deed for the sake of that deed alone.

The next week, on the morning of July 15th, I loaded my butchering supplies into the truck: chicken plucker, scalder, propane tanks and knives. Following the directions I had been given, I drove into the hills east of Homer to the Veteran's house. It was beautiful country. The day was already hot and would get hotter; 90+ degrees and humid. Butchering is hard work in any weather, and brutal in hot weather.

I was the first to arrive. I knocked on the house door. A home care worker greeted me and introduced me to Tommy, the Veteran who owned the chickens. He was sitting at his kitchen table smoking cigarettes. Soon his friend Dick showed up, and explained the situation. Some "friends" of Tommy's (who seemed more intent on taking advantage of him than helping him), had purchased the meat chickens as chicks in the spring, along with 50 laying hens. In prior years, Tommy had raised chickens. He owned a mobile poultry processing unit (an "MPPU," in the parlance of the American Pastured Poultry Association). This was a complete butchering operation on wheels, designed to be shared among small poultry growers.

After Tommy's friends convinced him to purchase the chicks, they were nowhere to be found when it came time to take care of them. It seemed they would show up from time to time to get money from Tommy to buy booze or whatever their habits needed, then would disappear. Tommy recently had his hip replaced and could barely walk, and the effects of the Agent Orange he was exposed to in Vietnam were growing progressively worse. Dick, his friend since high school, had stepped in to take care of the chickens, but he needed help to butcher them.

Dick and I left Tommy's house to set up the equipment for butchering. Tommy lived on a hillside, with his house at the top and a small garage/barn near the bottom of his few-acre property. The laying chickens were on the second floor of the barn, and the meat chickens were being pastured in two mobile boxes on the lawn. Beside the barn were the remains of Tommy's MPPU, which had been lent to someone who returned it with a caved-in roof. Its equipment had been rained on for years, and nettles and raspberries were growing up through its floor. It was useless, except for a plastic chill tank and three killing cones Dick and I dug out of the debris.

I went to work setting up the scalder and plucker

while Dick found some garden hose and ran it to where we would be working, in the shade on the north side of the barn. We bleached the chill tank and some cutting tables we found. Soon Anna arrived, and a man named Chris who lived in Cortland. None of us had known any of the others before today. We got started butchering.

It was a long day. The temperature went up and up and we were all covered in sweat. Dick did the killing, Anna the scalding and plucking, and Chris and I the gutting and dressing. We talked all day as we were working. Anna had a farm in Tully, north of Homer, that raised pork, beef, and lamb. Her husband did custom haying ("custom" means he hired out to other farms, cutting and baling their hay with his equipment). Chris was a landlord in Cortland, and owned quite a few commercial and residential properties.

Dick had quite a past. He had owned a few dairy farms, and worked for about five years for the State, under a grant to develop the pastured poultry industry. He had been involved with the APPA (American Pastured Poultry Association). He had helped develop prototypes for the MPPU, one of which Tommy owed. He had met Joel Salatin, a famous poultry farmer and early developer of modern pastured poultry grazing systems. And he had worked with Cornell University on developing better methods of rotational grazing for cattle. But here was his most important claim to fame: He had created the lyrics and music for the APPA theme song. He sung them to us from memory and we all had a good laugh. I'm still hoping to get him to sing it again one day so I can record it and write it down.

By 6pm we all had run out of energy. It was still hot. We had about 80 chickens in the chill tank, and 20 still in the pens. A couple times during the day, Tommy's deadbeat friends had stopped by, trying to take some of the chickens we had processed, claiming ownership because they had purchased the chicks. Dick angrily chased them off both times. We decided to leave the remaining 20. If Tommy's friends returned, they could purchase the live ones. We bagged the chickens we had finished and cleaned the equipment.

I pulled out of Tommy's driveway and drove home with the air conditioning on high. It had been a great day. I had met interesting people, heard many good stories, and helped someone in need. Not a dollar had been exchanged by anyone.

Dick visited me at the Homer market almost every week for the rest of the summer. Often we would talk for a half hour or more. Eventually Tommy's hip healed enough for him to come to the market with Dick, and he would sit on my big chicken cooler while we talked. Helping these friends out was one of the best things I did that summer. Although I had no return in mind, this charity put me on good footing for my entry into the Homer farming community.

Six

Rhythms: The sun's angle, the weather's bite, the garden's cycle. Repeating arcs, long and short. We are rhythmic; internal beats syncopating and disassociating with what surrounds us, synergy and discord. Never long at equilibrium; leaning and alive.

There is no stasis, no single arrangement to be sustained. There is only our harmonization with the ebb and flow of the systems surrounding us. A relationship is sustained and always in transition, rhythms searching for synchronization.

Rhythms move me; I am a passenger in transition. Though I long for my favorite phases in rhythm, I know they cannot be distinguished in stasis.

People tell me to flatten the rhythm. We can fix that now; leave the darkness for perpetual light. But I have reasons for letting the rhythms take me. The light is informed by the darkness, and the darkness by the light.

The world speeds toward homogenization. Find the optimal state and hold it, remove the peaks and valleys. Freeze appearances; stop the rhythms. Make a place the same as the other place and hold it in time, new. Accelerate toward timelessness.

I resist; I need the dark and the light. I want to be reborn with the spring, dream when the sun's high, fall inward, and let winter's low load the catapult for a new year's arc.

Age wears the sharp edges. When I was new I scraped the edges and knew I was alive, but experiences repeat into oblivion and the edges become smooth. What is left? There is no life in the optimal condition.

Rhythms remain, overlaid on one another, creating infinite combinations. The world is new.

-"Rhythms" December 2011

*   *   *

I was eight years old when my Grandfather died. He had been a woodsman all his life, working at the local lumber mill in addition to working the family farm. In his mid-seventies he was still cutting, hand splitting, and selling firewood for extra income. One day when I was in third grade he drove the tractor and wagon down to the east side of the woods to cut firewood. He cut down a tree that landed on one of its large lower branches. The branch acted as a large spring and flung the trunk back at him, crushing his pelvis.

By mid-afternoon, Mom was worried. From the kitchen window, she had seen Grandpa drive down to the woods, but she had not seen him return. Dad was working in his mechanic's shop next to their house.

Mom went out and asked him to go check on Grandpa. Dad walked down and found Grandpa slumped backward in the tractor seat, dead. Later his autopsy revealed he had drowned after he passed out - probably from the pain of his broken pelvis - and blood had filled his lungs. It was amazing he had the strength, probably without the use of his legs, to crawl back to the tractor and climb all the way up to its seat.

Dad walked back from the woods and called the ambulance. "No hurry," he said, "he's already dead." Dad asked me if I wanted to go down to the woods to see my grandfather. I didn't look at my Dad, I just said "no" as tears welled in my eyes and I struggled to see the toy helicopter I was stubbornly playing with on the stone fireplace hearth.

My Grandfather's death ripped a hole in my life. I had spent almost every day of my childhood with him. People tell me I have an old soul. I don't know if it's something I was born with, or the result of all the time I spent with my Grandfather. He was my link to my family's history; he was the fifth generation on our farm and I was the seventh. He could remember back to the third generation; Irving Miller, his Grandfather and my Great Great Grandfather, who had built our house and all the old barns. I wish I had learned more from him about those old relatives and the history of our place.

Grandpa was wise about time. His generation held the old perspective, the perspective I had discovered after I left work. He and I spent many hot summer afternoons doing nothing. It was an act, not of

73

laziness, but another form of meditation. It is a sage passing of time lost to all but a few today as the world mindlessly barrels ahead filled with stuff, shopping, overtime, soccer Moms and multitaskers.

*   *   *

In the 1880's, my great grandmother planted a horse chestnut tree in the backyard of our house. By the time I was eight, the tree was almost 100 years old and at least three feet in diameter at its furrowed base. I remember fragrant spring and hot summer afternoons spent under the tree with my Grandfather. We sat in steel chairs on the large slate flagstones of the walk that led from the back kitchen door, drinking water out of tin cups from the stone-lined well a few feet away. That water, ice-cold even in the hottest afternoons of summer, is the sweetest I ever drank.

We sat for hours, almost every day, under the horse chestnut: a living cathedral, its interior a leafless framework bounded by translucency. In the spring, thousands of bees came to work for weeks on the blossoms of the horse chestnut. Their drone rose through the morning and afternoon, then subsided and was replaced in the evening by the spring peepers in the swamp across the road. The sticky-sweet smell of the linen-white and pink chestnut blossoms mixed with the musty decay of the perpetually shaded kitchen wing of the old house and my grandfather's pipe as he lit another bowl of apple tobacco.

August's hot summer apex brought utility to shade.

We sat in the tree's dark coolness and listened to the piercing whines of the tree frogs. My grandfather told me this would be mine after he was gone. Time stopped and I needed to be nowhere.

The tree felt like a protector: strong, very old, alive, sheltering, rhythmic.

But it was gradually succumbing to horse chestnut blight, each leaf edged by brown deadness. Eventually, weakened in its resistance to the disease, the tree lost many of its branches to the wind. The cathedral's roof collapsed, and I cut its remains down in 2006. The base of its trunk measured 42" in diameter. A section of it hangs in my dining room, reminding me of its peace.

The next year, I planted a new horse chestnut tree.

*   *   *

Grandpa knew about the old cycles, the ones few pay attention to today. He watched the weather and knew when the elusive morels would appear after a particular sequence of rain and sunshine. He knew when the maple sap would start running and we tapped the trees in the woods with galvanized pipes and hung tin buckets with teepee lids to catch the sap and keep the rain out. He knew when to plant, when to harvest, and when to gather the wild foods growing around us, few of which we eat today: cowslips, morels, butternuts, black raspberries, puffballs, walnuts, on and on.

The modern world is collectively trying to flatten those cycles; pretend they're not there anymore. We are removing another source of richness and wonder from our lives in the name of efficiency and trying to hold the optimal state. The seasons' march, the sun's path, the moon's syncopation with the calendar, times of growth, harvest, and dormancy all repeating while we stare at the highway making our daily commute to work and back home.

The expenditure of energy is the cost of our flattening of natural cycles. Plowing the roads instead of taking a snow day. Conditioning buildings to 72 degrees year round. Waking and retiring at the same time all year, regardless of the sun's schedule. Buying fresh salad greens trucked from California in January.

When I was an architect I saw the same thing translated into discussions of building materials, following a simple equation:

$$\text{Control} = \text{Energy} = \text{Homogeneity} = \text{Waste}$$

The more we sought to control the "sameness" of one building part to another, the more material was wasted and the more energy we expended. It's no accident the most homogenous building materials are the most energy intensive to produce: steel, aluminum, glass, brick, and ceramic tile. These are the materials that require the most refinement: mining, melting, and forming.

The use of natural materials could exist as a low energy alternative to these high energy, industrial materials. But most designers missed that boat because of the values instilled in them in school. We were taught modern design architects could shamelessly control every detail, could even take one of nature's most wonderful qualities - its variability - and chop it, cut it, throw away and waste its undesirable parts to make it appear as a homogeneous, industrialized material. The best example of this is wood, almost always selected for its absence of knots and uniformity of grain, color, and piece size. Outside the back door of the mill lay the waste created by this attitude. This was another flattening of our wonderfully variable natural world.

I believe the flattening of natural cycles has affected our psychology too. Our bodies were meant to experience alternations of hard work and long quiet periods as the seasons passed. Modern life does not allow this, and some of us can't cope very well with the demands placed on us during the winter and the guilt associated with our natural impulse to slow down as the days get shorter. I experienced seasonal depression for years before I left the office world. I have felt little of it since I started farming and harmonized my pace to that of nature.

Once Grandpa opened my eyes to his world I never forgot it. When I left our farm for college and work in the city, a part of me went dormant, numb from the loss of my connection to natural cycles and nature's variability. Leaving office work and starting the farm woke my spirit again. It reconnected me to what was supposed to be; the symphony of overlapping rhythms and repeating cycles.

Life's cycles vary in duration. We often receive, and love to have, visitors to the farm. Our daughter, Grace, is the principle tour guide. One of the things we teach on our tours of the farm is how much farming is about learning to work with overlapping natural cycles and systems. The simplest example of this is the Cornish Cross, the most common meat chicken we raise.

Cornish Crosses live eight weeks. They are rockets through life...zero to eight pounds in 54 days. Amazing! Our tours of the farm walk the complete cycle of a meat chicken's life. We start at the brooders in the garage, where the chickens grow indoors for 14 to 21 days. Then we walk out to the pasture, where the chickens spend the remaining five or six weeks of their life, moving in pasture boxes along the fields. Finally, we come back around to the garage, which on its north end has the chicken butchering shed and inside, the coolers and freezers for storing processed chickens. Coincidentally, these refrigerators are near the brooders...a physical loop.

On any given day throughout the spring, summer, and fall, we have meat chickens on the farm at all stages of the cycle. Day old chicks come from the hatchery every two weeks, and every Wednesday we butcher mature chickens to bring them fresh to market. Meat chickens are unique this way; such a short lifecycle that visitors can understand their entire existence in one loop around the farm. We even walk them past the offal compost pile which turns chicken remains into rich black soil. One cycle ending and another beginning; life feeding life.

We also talk on the tour about our layer chickens, turkeys, and pigs, each of which has their own cycle of life. What is important to us, and what we want to show anyone who visits, is how each animal and the pasturing system mutually dependent to them create a single generative growth system, making our farm healthier year after year. It's no coincidence that I focus so much on system and cycle, Grandpa taught me this. I had only forgotten it for thirty-five years.

After Grandpa died, I would not enter the woods for a year or more; I don't remember exactly how long. Dad took the tractor back down and cut up the tree that had killed Grandpa; it must have been a hard thing to do but I would not help him. Grandpa had been cutting on the edge of the woods, the most dangerous place to fell trees, the place of the widow makers. Trees in the middle of the woods typically grow straight and tall, and lose their lower branches as they became shaded by other trees. But trees on the edge of the woods hold their lower branches facing the field, and these branches often grow large and horizontal as the tree searches for more sunlight. When such a tree is cut, it will fall toward the field, onto its large lower branches, and often roll or spring back, as in the way Grandpa was killed.

I still cut firewood from our woods; our house is heated with wood from our land, and I have cut trees from its edges. It seems to me that a woodsman rolls the dice every morning he enters the woods; sooner or later, he encounters a tree with his destiny written in its branches.

Over the years following Grandpa's death, I occasionally visited the stump of the tree that had killed him. I watched it gradually rot back into the soil over the decades, until one day I went looking for it and found nothing but leaves in its place. My Grandfather's destiny was one with that tree, he in his grave and its stump rotting in the woods. Both the tree and my Grandfather shared the same cycle of life, the tree sprouting in the forest very near the time he was born in 1901, and its remains feeding the saplings sprouting from the seeds it had dropped around it. My grandfather had nourished me during his life as the saplings were nourished, teaching me about time and cycle in the old ways, leaving an indelible print on my soul that would in turn determine my destiny to rediscover life on the farm.

Seven

By March I had been away from architecture for a month, drifting along, going to the auction and working on old clocks. During this time I was keeping in touch with a few close friends from the firm.

Every week, I went to visit Deborah and Bob Rhea. Deborah was the firm's CFO (chief financial officer), and a strong advocate for the design philosophy I was developing when I worked there. Deborah had worked in Europe and in South America for the State Department and Boston University. She and Bob had lived overseas and raised their two sons in Switzerland, Belgium, and Guyana before coming back to the States about five years ago.

There was a reason we held our weekly schedule: Deborah was our egg courier to the firm. We had a dozen laying hens, and while I was working at the firm, I sold our extra eggs to my coworkers. This continued after I left via Deborah, who lived about halfway between our farm and the firm.

Sometimes the Rheas would make dinner for me. They were both excellent cooks. We ate, talked, and drank for a few hours each visit. This was an important therapy for me. They were most concerned about how I was doing; my moods as I wandered through this period; what I thought I might do with my future. They were passionate people who had the perspective of a rich life, and they believed in me. I valued their advice.

Deborah is a problem solver. Any issue, any mood I brought she tried to solve by the end of my visit. It seemed every visit had a theme. Often it was exercise and diet as the cure for my mood, "Get out and ski! Start the South Beach diet!" She had good intentions but often the subject of the night had no simple cure. One evening in March I began talking about some vague ideas I had for restarting the farm. This had been simmering since before I left work.

That night, March tenth, is a bright clear spot in my memory, a night that changed everything to come. I had brought my seven year old daughter Grace with me, and she munched cookies and sipped honey-sweetened tea as we all sat around Deborah's dining room table, politely listening as our conversation turned to farming. "Grow pastured chicken!" Deborah exclaimed, "Farm the way Joel does!" In their travels, Deborah and Bob had been neighbors and friends with Joel Salatin in Swoope, Virginia, and had purchased their meat from him. Joel had pioneered a way of pasturing chickens, turkeys, rabbits, cattle and pork such that each animal became part of a mutually beneficial, generative system. He and his father had started with about 500 acres of exhausted land devoid of topsoil in some places, abused by hundreds of years of irresponsible farming practices, and turned that land into an intensely productive livestock farm. Deborah had introduced me to Joel's methods years ago, and I admired them, but I was vague about the details.

Deborah and Bob were convinced there was a huge, unfilled local demand for pastured meat, principally chicken. Bob in particular knew the local food scene, as he traveled from market to market and farm to farm to gather their groceries. They had been locavores ever since living next to the Salatins. But pastured chicken was spotty in this area. Farms would butcher once a month, and you had to go to the farm to pick up your chickens on butchering day, or you would have to wait until the next month. Sometimes pastured chicken was sold at the local farmers markets, but again there was no consistency. If we could provide a dependable, constant supply, Deborah was sure customers would be lining up outside our door. That night Grace and I left Deborah's and Bob's house with an armload of Salatin's how-to books; Deborah had his complete library.

Something clicked in me that night, the beginnings of a direction that became a consuming passion to prove our small farm could generate enough income to modestly support our family while at the same time improving its land year by year. I would start with raising broiler chickens. When I got home I carefully studied the photos and descriptions of Joel's mobile pasture pens in his book, "Pastured Poultry Profits."

The next day I went to the local lumberyard and purchased the materials needed to build a ten foot by twelve foot mobile broiler pen. Dad and I went to the steelyard to purchase tube steel to build the wheeled dolly to move the boxes. By the end of the day I had the framing of the first box screwed together in one bay of our garage. By the end of the week the first broiler pen, and a mobile pen for our laying chickens, were finished and out on the pasture. Exactly one month after that night at the Rheas' - April tenth - we picked up our first fifty broiler chickens at the local Agway.

During this period Hil and I were also making plans for other livestock. We ordered three piglets from a local breeder, to be picked up in mid-April. We fenced a pasture for them in a brushy area behind the pole barn and built a shelter for them. We planned to take advantage of their plowing services to clear the area, just as Joel Salatin used pigs' plowing services to aerate soil and barn bedding. We ordered a dozen turkeys. And we started expanding our layer flock, purchasing about sixty chicks through the mail. We were moving fast. I had no reservations, was excited and even obsessed with, our direction.

In April we settled on our farm's name: Just a Few Acres, and we created our website, justafewacres.com. This led us to create statements about what made our farm unique and what its philosophy was. We were proud of our family lineage and connection to place; that we were the seventh generation of our family on the land, living here since 1804. We cared about the land's long term health, hopefully for future generations of our family to continue the farm. The website highlighted these things.

One of the first posts on the farm website we called our Manifesto, a vision and six statements regarding the ethics of our farming practices. These have served us well so far, guiding our decisions regarding the farm's development.

The vision is of land glowing with health, covered with green pastures and animals grazing, with replanted hedgerows; narrow ecotones teeming with life. It's also a systems model, overlapping plant and animal systems that are mutually beneficial; where the animals improve their pasture every year, and in turn the pasture can support more animals every year. Poultry and ruminants (cows and sheep) work well to do this, if they are used together. Cows in an intensive grazing arrangement, moved every few days, broiler chickens and turkeys in mobile pens grazing near the cattle, taking advantage of the fine, tender, and low forage, and laying chickens moving after the cattle, taking larvae from fresh cattle manure and spreading the manure in the process. I learned these things from reading Joel Salatin's books and watching his lectures online.

Now to the ethic. Although this was an old family farm, we were newbie livestock farmers with an intentional naiveté about conventional practices, and I was fond of moving against the grain in most all things. Note the word *ethic*...We thought of this as a morality; a set of ideals to strive toward; a value set to

85

base everyday decisions upon. I couldn't say we'd nailed every one, but we were using them to guide our decision making. There were six:

#1: **Carry NO debt**...no mortgage, no machinery loans, no vehicle loans, no credit cards. We believe there was no such thing as "good debt." This attitude was one of the reasons the farm had remained in our family for so long. We would scrounge and reuse. And we would grow our farm with cash instead of credit.

#2: **Maintain almost no machinery.** Livestock appreciates and machinery depreciates. We didn't have the money to accommodate such expenditures. Our small livestock farm hadn't enough land to grow our own feed crops, which eliminated the need for all the specialized machinery associated with them: plows, planters, combines, etc. This aligned with our goal to minimize fossil-fuel use, and our wish to grow the health of the land through minimal topsoil disturbance, preserving the important life systems occupying the top few inches of the earth.

We thought of the land we owned as a bank of stored nutrients. We were better off spending our money importing nutrients from other farms in the form of hay and grains, instead of buying equipment and using it to export nutrients from our farm (in the form of meat). We would thus be adding to our farm's nutrient bank via the feed conversion ratio of our livestock. For example, if I was buying grain to feed chickens that have a feed conversion ratio between 2:1 and 3:1, then ½ to 2/3 of the nutrients I imported to the farm via feed were added to the farm's nutrient bank via chicken manure.

We already owned most of the machinery we would need. It consisted of three old Farmall tractors in the twenty to thirty horsepower range. Mostly they would be used to tow things around the farm: mobile feed storage bins, wagons, and chicken coops. We also owned implements for mowing, snow plowing, and digging post holes. Looking into the future, we knew we would need a loader for one of the tractors. But we could get along without that for now.

#3: **Make all infrastructure adaptable and portable.** Our pasturing plans brought the livestock to the feed (pasture), instead of the opposite; often the case in industrial farming. The exception was poultry, which would still require feed to supplement their grazing. Bringing the livestock to the feed meant our infrastructure: fences, shelters, the water supply, supplemental poultry feed, laying houses, and pasture pens, must be able to be easily moved on a daily basis, preferably without a tractor. And our infrastructure should be adaptable to our increasing knowledge of best practice. As we learned, we could reconfigure our farm to work better.

#4: **Prioritize expenses not income.** The dollar not spent is the dollar earned. We had to learn to be more thrifty. We had already minimized our expenses by using solar electricity to power our home, cutting firewood to heat it, growing some of our own food, and paying off our debts. This examination of overhead needed to continue into the realm of livestock production.

#5: **Output per acre and overlapping systems.**
Farm land is usually neatly divided according to
purpose: hayfield, pig pen, cow pasture, corn field,
chicken coop. Joel Salatin works his farm as a
symphony conductor would: moving livestock around
multipurpose pastures. Cattle, chickens, turkeys, and
pigs moved daily to take best advantage of the
pasture's forage height and the livestock that would
come before and after them. He had proven that
when properly practiced, such intensive pasture use
could increase the output of the pasture year after
year.

#6: **Speak ill of others only to family.** Never
spread gossip.

Later we would add two more statements:

#7: **Work to increase the long term health of
the land and the community.** The increasing health
of the land was implicit in the previous statements,
but we felt it was so important it should have its own
place. Tied to our land's health was the health of the
community we lived in, through the healthy
nutritional qualities (vs. industrial farming) of the
livestock we grew, and by purchasing our supplies
locally, supporting and adding to the community's
economic health with our business.

#8: **Create direct relationships with end
consumers.** We operated "farm to table." We
formed direct relationships with the people who
consumed our products, with no intermediaries. This
ethic gave us the opportunity to educate consumers
about how their food was grown and its differences
from industrial farming, straight from the horse's

mouth, so to speak. This, like ethic #7, also worked to build stronger ties within our community.

Looking back, Hil and I were amazed at the speed with which we made decisions that April. I think my heritage had finally caught up with me; the seeds my Grandfather had planted long ago were finally germinating.

Still, I wondered about my future in architecture, and the coexistence of my old career with farming after my six month leave was over. I placed that at the back of my mind with some confidence my path would become clear when the time was right.

Eight

The most difficult part of raising livestock is butchering. Some call it "processing," as in "we're processing chickens today." This statement takes feeling out of the act; treats killing like a manufacturing operation. We butcher our animals.

Butchering is emotional. It is one being killing another. It is pain, blood, and guts. It's messy. It's the part of farming few consumers want to see. And it's the most guarded, brutal, and inhumane part of the industrial meat production system.

Butchering chickens and turkeys ourselves, on the farm, was the logical thing for us to do. It kept the entire production process under our oversight, helping us to ensure the most humane treatment of our animals and a top quality product. And, not hiring a butcher helped to maximize our profit.

I knew what I was getting into. When I was a kid butchering on the farm was a part of life. Every Fall, when the temperature was right for curing meat, we butchered pigs and cows. Each was difficult in its own way. The pigs were shot, their throat artery cut (called "sticking" a pig) to bleed them out, then scalded. Scalding was the dipping of the carcass in hot water to loosen its hair or feathers. Early in the morning on pig butchering day, we would turn over the giant cast iron scalding pot (a half sphere about five feet in diameter) near the pig pen. The pot, due to its weight, was left in the same place all year, and simply turned upside-down when not in use, to keep rain out. Once it was turned right side up it was filled with water and a wood fire built around its base to warm the water. A floating thermometer let us know when the water reached 160 degrees, optimal scalding temperature. This took most of the morning. Oak planks were laid up to the edge of one side of the pot, forming a ramp, up which the pig was dragged with hooks in its mouth, for dunking into the water. A flat plank table, held up by sawhorses, was erected on the other side of the pot. Once the pig was scalded it was dragged out of the pot and onto this table, where its loosened hair was scraped off with round bell scrapers. The pigs weighed around 300 pounds, and it took three or four men to perform the scalding operation. Once the pig was scalded, it was hung by making slits through the skin between its rear foot bones and tendons, and inserting a straight piece of wood called a singletree between its rear legs. The singletree had an iron ring at its center, and this was attached to a rope and pulleys, usually tossed over a strong tree limb. Thus the pig was hoisted up to finish its bleed-out and evisceration. It would hang for days to cure the meat before it was ready to be cut up.

Butchering cows was a simpler process, as they were skinned of their hides instead of scalded. Their weight, sometimes as much as 2,000 pounds, was the main difficulty. They were shot, bled, hung, eviscerated, and skinned, then left to cure as the pigs were. Moving and hanging their carcasses was not easy, usually requiring the assistance of a tractor.

After they had cured, cutting and packaging the carcass was an event that brought our extended family together - usually about ten relatives - for the job, which lasted most of the day. My mother's uncle Roy Palmer was expert at cutting up all types of livestock, and directed the operation. Roles were dependent on gender and age back then. The men quartered the carcass and brought it into Dad's garage, then cut it up on makeshift tables. A lot of knowledge was required to identify how to cut the carcass properly into familiar steaks, chops, roasts, etc. Hamburger was also ground in the garage. Children carried the cut meat into the house in large metal bowls. In the house, the women wrapped the meat in butcher paper and masking tape, and wrote the cut and the date on the package.

At the end of the day, everyone left with some meat of their own as payment for their work. If the day's work was pork, Uncle Roy left with the hams and bellies (bacon), which he would smoke in a wooden smokehouse behind his home and bring back a few weeks later.

I have good memories of those butchering days.

They brought family together, provided our food, and were understood as part of the cycle of life. Animals were killed humanely with a single shot in the brain. I saw little suffering. As time went on, my parents quit doing their own butchering, opting to send their livestock to a local butcher instead. I'm not sure why they made this change, it may have been the amount of work required. But as Dad and I hunted deer, we continued our own butchering of game. Thus I felt prepared to take on the butchering of our chickens and turkeys.

Poultry farming is unique in that small farms are still permitted to butcher on the farm without constructing an expensive facility, if they follow some simple guidelines (an important one is the farmer has to sell their products directly to the end consumer). Farms raising all other types of meat have to have their livestock trucked to a butcher that employs a USDA (United States Department of Agriculture) inspector. Their meat comes back packaged with a USDA stamp on the label, and then can be sold to supermarkets, restaurants, and consumers. Butchers, unfortunately, have become like feed mills: there used to be one in every town and now they are getting hard to find. Increasingly demanding federal requirements have put many out of business. The economies of scale and centralization have closed others.

In April, at about the same time as we purchased our first batch of Cornish Cross meat chickens, we began to learn all the government requirements, and to collect the equipment needed, for our first butchering day coming in two months. We needed killing cones, a scalder, a feather plucker, sink, coolers, shrink bags, and the proper government required labels.

We borrowed a turkey fryer from my parents to use as a scalder, and a large cooler to quickly chill the dressed chickens in. I made killing cones out of aluminum sheet stock from a pattern I found online, and bought a used porcelain coated steel sink with drainboards at a local building parts salvage store. I went looking online for a feather plucker. Commercial units cost upwards of $1,500. Could I find a used one? No luck there. On one of my searches, a do-it-yourself machine called the "Whizbang Chicken Plucker" popped up. It was a plucker built by mounting a cut-off plastic drum in a wood frame, with an electric motor-powered rotating aluminum disc in the bottom of the drum, covered with rubber fingers to remove the feathers. To make construction easier, the inventor sold a kit containing the harder-to-find parts: the rubber plucker fingers, the pulleys and shafts, the rotating aluminum disc, and a book detailing the plucker's construction. I read testimonials on other websites about how well the plucker worked and saw videos of it in action. I could build this plucker for less than half the price of the commercial units.

Amazingly, the inventor, Herrick Kimball, lived only a few towns away. I called him up and arranged to visit his home to pick up his deluxe kit. I had read so much about the popularity of his blogs and inventions on the internet that I felt I was going to see a sort of poultry celebrity (however, the title of

95

"the chicken man" had already been claimed by a man who owned a poultry supply business downstate from us).

I pulled into his driveway and looked around. He lived in a small house with a small, adjoining workshop, on a few acres of land. He was an "intensive homesteader," growing as much of his food as he could on his land and supplementing his income with the internet sales of his inventions; not only the chicken plucker, but also an automatic scalder made from a cut off gas fired water heater, and various designs for portable pasture shelters and hand powered carts.

Herrick had just made the leap from teaching woodworking at a nearby state prison to working full-time at his home-based business. We shared some conversation about that, as I was starting to dwell on similar thoughts regarding the farm. I left with the plucker kit and some free shrink bags for packaging chicken.

The plucker was fun to build. Herrick's book was a great how-to guide, and in a few days I had the plucker finished. We were ready for our first butcher day, still some weeks away.

I had never butchered a chicken before; I had only dim memories of Grandpa butchering a few and plucking them by hand. Herrick's blog really helped me out. In his usual meticulous fashion, he had written a post that had step-by-step instructions for butchering, accompanied by helpful photographs. A lot of people must have run into the same questions I had about butchering, because the post had received over a million hits.

On the morning of May 30th, I went outside at 5:30am and started setting up to butcher in our woodshed. The woodshed was open on three sides, with the fourth butting up to the back of the garage. This was the perfect place: it had a metal roof to keep sun and rain out, a gravel floor to drain any water we spilled, and excellent ventilation from the predominant northwest winds. I agreed wholeheartedly with Joel Salatin's opinion that outdoor butchering was much more sanitary than indoor butchering. Nature was the best cleaning service we could have. Assuming we butchered once per week, the rest of the week ultraviolet light from the sun would kill lingering bacteria and rain would wash the ground clean. While butchering, the breeze also served to carry away airborne contaminants. Enclosed butchering buildings serve to concentrate pathogens, just as hospitals do. The only way to ensure either is pathogen-free was a perfect cleaning regimen, unachievable of course.

This is not to say we threw blood, guts, and feathers everywhere for nature to take care of! We collected the viscera in buckets and composted it behind the barn, adding fresh wood mulch on top of each layer of chicken offal. Eventually this would become rich soil for the garden. We carefully scrubbed and bleached all our equipment. Some things, like the sink, scalding pot, and chill tank, were bleached multiple times in a single day. We were careful to keep bleach off the chicken carcasses by thoroughly rinsing the equipment after bleaching.

At 7:00am everything was ready to go. We would be butchering 27 Cornish Cross chickens. Only 27 had survived from our original 50, because of my mistake of allowing them to eat as much feed as they wanted. Cornish Cross' feed needs to be rationed, or else they eat themselves to death via congestive heart failure. Only 27 chickens I thought, I'll be done by the end of the morning. How many did Salatin butcher in a day? 450? I had arranged for customers to pick up all the packaged chickens in mid-afternoon.

By 10am I knew I had miscalculated. It had taken me three hours to butcher 10 chickens. The temperature outside was on its way up to 90 degrees and the humidity was becoming oppressive. Despite my previous butchering experience the sights, smells, and heat were making me queasy. I thought the process through to see if I was getting hung up in any particular area...and found there were inefficiencies all over the place.

First of all, I had not gathered the chickens the night before. Instead, I attached a small wagon with a plastic storage bin in it to the lawn tractor and went out to the pasture to collect six chickens at a time. I had to crawl into the pasture box (the worst task in the 90 degree heat), and grab the chickens one-by-one, putting them into the plastic bin with the lid on and bringing them back to the shed. There they would suffer in the heat of the sealed bin until their time came.

The next steps were going pretty smoothly. From the bin the chickens were taken, two at a time, and placed head down in the killing cones. The artery and vein in their necks were slit and they bled to death into buckets beneath. They did not seem to suffer much. From here they were dipped into the 145 degree water of the scalder until their feathers could be pulled out easily (less than a minute). The plucker worked wonderfully, taking all the feathers off the chickens in about twenty seconds. My Grandpa would have liked to have had one of these machines!

Next, the featherless carcasses were thoroughly rinsed and placed on the sink drain boards. When six birds accumulated I finished dressing them: cut off the heads and feet, removed the crop at the base of the neck, and cut off the neck. To eviscerate them, I made a small slit just above their rear vent (manure and egg exit hole), widened the slit with my fingers, and pulled the entrails out of the hole. Lastly, the bright pink lungs had to be pulled from the rib cage near the front of the chicken. All along these steps, the carcasses were rinsed with copious amounts of fresh water.

Two things were slowing the dressing of the chickens: The five gallon water bucket I had placed under the sink drain had to be emptied after every two or three chickens were finished, carried across the lawn and dumped in a different place every time. And I was almost to the point of pulling my fingernails loose when trying to get all the bits of lung away from the rib cages.

I bulled ahead, determined to finish all the birds that day. Setup, cleanup, and teardown are half of the work on butcher day, and I did not want to repeat those processes for just a few birds the next day. By

4pm I had all the chickens in the chill tank, which had been filled with cold water and ice made by freezing gallon milk jugs full of water. Dad had come over to give me a hand with the last six chickens. The heat and humidity had become practically unbearable. We weren't nearly done, though: We had to clean up before we could shrink-bag the chickens. We had to clean all the feathers out of the plucker. We had to carry the buckets of entrails, feathers, and blood to the compost pile. We had had to scrub and bleach all the buckets, the scalding pot, the sink, and the knives and thermometer.

After this, it was time to bag. Hilarie came to help with this part. We filled the clean scalding pot with fresh water and heated it to 180 degrees. Once again in groups of six, we pulled the chickens out of the chill tank and gave them a final rinse and quality-control inspection; looking for any remaining feathers, bits of entrails, etc. We then let them drip-dry for about five minutes, slipped shrink bags over the head-end of each, and shrunk the bag to fit by dipping the bagged chicken in the hot water. Hilarie then took the bagged chickens to the refrigerator in the garage. Finished!

It was now 8pm. We had butchered 27 chickens in 13 hours. All along the way I had underestimated how long the process would take. At 4 o'clock and 6 o'clock I had phoned our customers, advising them of the delay. Now they arrived and bought all the chicken, leaving one for us. I was exhausted.

As Hilarie and I relaxed that evening, I felt proud. We had done it: grown our first batch of chickens from one day old chicks to ready-to-cook, dressed chickens. I was nervous about how they would taste, and would have to wait for the feedback of those that had purchased them.

When I added up our expenses and income a few days later, I found we had made 50 dollars from those first 27 chickens, excluding our labor. I wasn't alarmed by this dismal profit. We would cut our mortality rate and reduce our feed costs by adhering to a strict feeding regimen, and we would improve our butchering efficiency. As the summer progressed and we grew about a dozen more batches of chickens, my assumptions proved themselves: our mortality rate dropped to less than 5%, our feeding regimen became very efficient, and our butchering streamlined. Our broiler business would prove to be nicely profitable. We also received rave reviews on the flavor of the first batch; so important to the growth of our business.

In later batches, I solved the butchering inefficiencies of the first. I made a set of plywood paddles which, when inserted and swept around the inside of the pasture box, collected the chickens in one quadrant of the box with minimal stress. I built a four foot by eight foot wagon dubbed the "chicken mobile," which was a humane place for chickens to wait on butchering day, complete with shade and water. The evening before butchering day, I would collect the chickens into the wagon and park it around the corner of the garage, out of sight of the butchering operation. Reducing the chickens' stress prior to butchering was important to me from both an ethical standpoint and a quality standpoint; I felt stress at the end of an animal's life affected the quality of its meat.

I eliminated using a drain bucket under the sink by making a moveable drain out of a ten foot long pipe and a no-hub rubber elbow fitting. This slipped onto the sink drain on butchering day and could be moved to distribute waste water onto the lawn in different places. Lastly, I made a lung pulling tool after looking at photos of ones for sale on the internet.

Most of all, our butchering efficiency increased through practice. For much of the summer we butchered chickens on a weekly basis, timed so we could bring both fresh and frozen chickens to the weekly markets. We usually butchered 30 chickens per day. By the end of the season we would have them all in the chill tank by lunchtime, and bagged and in the refrigerator by 2pm.

Although my queasiness is long gone, I never quit feeling the emotional aspects of butchering, never reduced it to the mechanical "processing" some others may feel. Butchering is a necessary and serious act that should be handled with respect. I felt this most strongly when I held a chicken's legs as its life passed away in the killing cone; could sense its departure and its final peace. Death is a necessary part of life. Each chicken gave its life for our sustenance. We were proud to be able to give our chickens the best quality of life and the most humane death possible. We were proud to tell our customers their chickens were ethically raised and butchered.

Nine

May came and I was busy. We had our first batch of chickens on pasture and I was getting ready for the arrival of more; building pasture boxes, setting up the winter chicken coop as a brooder house (until it later became the home of our young layers and the brooders moved into the garage), and getting the pigs' shelter ready for their arrival.

At the same time, I was taking care of our customary May chores: planting garden greens and getting ready for the late-May planting of summer crops, cleaning up the perennial beds, and mulching the young trees in the back fields.

And, picking dandelions! Hilarie and I had big plans for dandelion wine this year...then we realized how many dandelions we needed to pick. We tried to convince the kids how exciting the work was (singing "My Momma had a baby and its head popped off" as we popped the blossom from its stalk into the big bowl). We didn't do a very good job of selling it…soon the kids were back in the sandbox or bicycling up and down the driveway. Maybe we would have had better luck if we'd promised them a share of the wine. We managed to collect enough dandelion heads for eight gallons, or 40 wine bottles; a respectable harvest.

To manage all the work, I had a prioritized to-do list on my smart phone; every day I made goals for tasks to be completed. As the sun rose earlier and earlier each morning, I rose earlier and earlier. I loved the work; my imagination saw the vegetable garden flourishing as I planted it, imagined hundreds of chickens on the pasture and every beautiful, sunny day I would be spending outside as spring led to summer.

With all this work, I sometimes forgot one of the main aspects of my new life as a farmer: the importance of doing the chores both looking up and looking down. Joel Salatin talked of this in one of his books. I had a lot of jobs to take care of, and I enjoyed doing my work, but I could never forget *why* I loved what I was doing; could never forget to look up to see the wonders of nature's office in which I had the privilege of working. It took my son to remind me of this.

Henry was four years old, fascinated with all things that rolled or floated, and quite a resourceful little guy. I imagine his resourcefulness was, in part, a product of having two older and more vocal sisters. Henry was also one of the finest observers I had ever met. When given a mechanical toy, or even watching me work on a clock mechanism, he would carefully watch, turn the object around and work its parts if he was allowed, and explain to me the basics of how their mechanisms worked. We spent evenings taking his motorized toys apart, figuring out how they worked, and then putting them back together again. I believed knowing how to repair things was an important skill rapidly fading in an age of disposability. Many things which could be repaired ended up in landfills. Henry's mechanical aptitude gave me hope.

Our garage is behind the house and a short sidewalk connects the two. That May, I marched the sidewalk many times, intent on my trips back and forth from the house to the garage and vice versa, completing the items on my to-do list. One Saturday, I marched up the sidewalk and found Henry crouched at its bend, intently observing something on the walk.

A few times every spring and summer, tiny ants about an eighth of an inch long crossed from one side of our sidewalk to the other. This was a journey of about four feet (a few miles in ant-distance?). They took everything they owned, which is to say themselves and their young, and they went from the left side to the right side of the sidewalk. There were thousands of them, so many and so small that, in passing, they looked like a dark stain on the sidewalk. I had never seen them cross from right to left, nor did I know if they were the same ants year to year. I also did not know why they did it; I chalked it up to their believing, as many of us do, that the grass is greener on the other side! This crossing took all day. The sidewalk was made of concrete bricks, not easy for something so small to navigate.

Henry was stand-sitting, as only little kids can, with the flats of his feet and his butt on the ground at the same time, watching them. Henry, being four, did not stay in any one place for long, but here he was, intently watching the ant crossing. Henry had other important things to do on that nice May day; sticks to drag out from the brush lot at the edge of the yard to whack things with, canals to make in the sandbox, and interesting rocks to bring into the house from the driveway. But throughout the day he remembered what the ants were up to and came back to check on their progress.

I wouldn't have paused for this event without Henry. I was doing my chores "looking down." My attention was fixed on the next task - not on the now - and it took Henry's view of the world to alter mine. With his simple act of stopping his activities to watch the ants, Henry taught me to take a breath, linger, and see as he does. I couldn't have done that three months ago, but now with my new perspective of life's priorities, I was happy to do so.

At four years old, Henry still felt the world's novelty. He was learning the world moment by moment, encounter by encounter. He was learning it through the things he could experience with his own senses, not via what others told him. Thus, every relationship he made was genuine and true to him; no one told him the ants were an unimportant detail in life, and no one told him to believe a certain way other than the opinions he formed through his own experiences.

I admired my son for his stubborn conviction to experience the world on his own terms, not settling to be told how things worked. He had to see it for himself. I wanted him to question everything. Oh, and he was stubborn; a blessing and a curse as a parent! I was proud of him for it; would tolerate his future teachers' notices of non-conformity in school. Go Henry! Have the confidence to challenge convention!

Henry's attitude would require Hilarie's and my support. I resolved to help my son to stay true to his own experience when the world of public education came crashing in and pressured him to conform. I wished for him a stubborn independence to meet the world in his own way, according to his own experience.

On that day in May, I stopped my march up the walk, and knelt with my son. I looked up by looking down. I put my arm on Henry's shoulder and we watched. Why was there a battle occurring in the middle of the walk? Was this an annual feud between two rival colonies? Was a new queen splitting off from the original colony? Henry and I did not know, but we had the time to watch, together. We did not need answers.

I looked up at the sky and felt fortunate to have the ability to pause and see through my son's eyes; that I was not 50 miles away sitting at a desk. I hoped my and Henry's ancestors could see our lives slowing to see what they had seen in their day, and that they would be proud as I was. Almost anything could wait until the next day as I floated down time's river.

That afternoon I managed to get the garden tilled. In the evening I barbecued hamburgers and hot dogs on our charcoal grill. Hil and I preferred charcoal grilling to gas. The flavor had no comparison; we may as well cook the burgers in a frying pan if we used a gas grill. Dad and I had a large pile of hickory cordwood in the pole barn, and once this was split, soaked in water, and added to the coals, true barbecue nirvana was achieved.

Barbecuing is a father's secret retreat. Well, not really secret...Hilarie could see me out the mudroom window, but at the end of the day, when I needed some quiet time, she graciously kept the kids inside while I enjoyed a beer or two sitting near the grill. The grill was kept in the woodshed and pulled out into the lawn when in use. I sat in a lawn chair, with my feet on another, looking up at the breeze in the tree branches, and back at the house and the perennial beds sprouting around it, as the charcoal warmed up in the grill's chimney.

Grace came out and I pulled another chair next to mine for her. I was glad Grace had come out. She was seven years old, had innate social skills and a quick intelligence; an ability to fit into any social setting and a broad curiosity about everything around her. Funny how a parent recognizes a child's strengths early; Grace was talking at 18 months and the best cuddler of any of our children. We knew she would do well in whatever environment she was placed in. Grace and I sat and looked at the fire warming up, and at the coop garden I had just put in.

Last summer and winter our dozen laying chickens had the run of a sixteen by twenty foot outdoor area, fenced with six foot tall welded wire. After the first month all the grass was gone. The chickens dug in the soil, looking for bugs and worms, and made holes to take dirt baths in, which helped rid them of skin parasites. Needless to say, they pooped a great deal in the run. Now they were out on pasture. I thought of all the nitrogen-rich soil their manure had left behind in the run, and decided to plant a garden there. I focused on greens: arugula, Simpson lettuce, Waldmann's lettuce, romaine, and mustard. I also planted pole beans, peas, beets, radishes, and summer squash. I rabbit-proofed the garden with hardware cloth one foot high, and laid down soaker hoses along the rows. To reduce weeding, I placed cardboard with wood mulch on top between the rows.

When the chickens moved back into their winter quarters, the cycle would complete itself. They would eat any of the remaining greens, and work the carbon-rich wood mulch into the soil, at the same time applying another layer of nitrogen rich chicken poop to the whole thing and creating an even more fertile garden for next year. These types of synergies, in this case between poultry and vegetables, were like magic to me. Here we had two systems that benefitted each other with little work on my part. I was just a conductor; getting the right plants and animals into the right places at the right times. My goal was to find more of these synergies.

Grace and I looked at the greens sprouting in the coop garden, and I told her of the complementary relationship between the chickens and the garden. She understood the "poop = good soil" part of the description. I was happy with that. When I was an architect, I worked with kids and adults who had never planted a seed and knew nothing about soil fertility. I urged them to plant something, anything, and care for it as the first step in understanding how to live a more environmentally responsible life. To many, nature's working had become mysterious. The farm was starting to give our kids the most important sort of education; how the cycles of life and its nutrients worked.

The fire was ready. I dumped the chimney full of charcoal and spread out the glowing pieces; put the cooking grate in and the burgers and hot dogs on, then closed the lid. Soon the grill was shooting delicious smelling smoke out its top damper. I had burgers and dogs down to a science; we would rather eat our own than any $15 burger at a Manhattan restaurant.

Grace and I finished the meat and brought it into the house. We had fresh asparagus from our 60 plant bed in the garden, and Hilarie had made rhubarb cobbler for dessert; also from the garden and my favorite. Hilarie and I believed the sharing of family dinners were an inviolable routine: the TV went off, all kids were to eat at the dining room table, no toys were allowed, and the food was to have meaning; grown by us or locally. Talk was to be of the day's activities; what the kids had done at school and what was happening on the farm. On weekdays, dinner was the only time all five of us were together.

Sunday morning dawned. It was another beautiful May day. I put on my barn boots and headed out to the pasture to feed the meat chickens and move their pasture boxes. I also fed the laying chickens in their pasture box, and moved them to new pasture. The laying chickens' box was equipped with four nesting boxes hung from its top, accessible by a hinged door covered with corrugated steel roofing. Our six Rhode Island Red hens, five white leghorn hens, and one white leghorn rooster (named "Rooster Cogburn") occupied this box. Our laying flock would expand dramatically later in the year, but for now, it was only these eleven layers and one pompous rooster.

The layers were over a year old, and had reliably laid ten or eleven eggs every day since reaching maturity, even through the dark winter. Since putting them on pasture in April, the quality off their eggs had changed dramatically. I had never seen eggs like these; thick whites and bright orange yolks. The supermarkets offered nothing close to the quality of these eggs.

Our ten year old daughter Cora knew our layer flock better than anyone. She visited them every day. When they were in the coop near the house, Cora would sit just outside the fence, pick grass from the lawn, and feed it to the chickens through the fence. Now that they were out on the pasture, Cora would walk out and sit by the box, feeding the chickens the same way. She would even do this on weekdays before the school bus came.

Cora knew each chicken by name (she and Grace had named them the summer before: Pony, Barbie,

Auntie Em, Peach, Fluffy Butt, Flo, Dragon, etc.). I hadn't taken the time to notice the nuances in the chickens' appearances to tell them apart, but Cora knew them each as she would another person. And she knew their personalities. Barbie was a pristine, lily white leghorn with tall, straight tail feathers. She avoided the mud and chicken poop that always wound up on the other chickens; truly a princess. Barbie was Cora's favorite (named after Cora's infatuation with Barbie dolls, which followed her love for Spongebob Squarepants and preceded her preoccupation with Fairies).

Cora sat and talked to the layers as a mother to her children, admonishing them to behave and treat each other with courtesy ("Flo, quit stealing grass from Fluffy Butt!"). Cora had some troubles with socialization at school. Here was a little society she could participate in without the complexities of the 'tween set at school to which she belonged. She talked to the chickens as she would other children, and I think the chickens appreciated her attention. In turn, Cora was developing her skills of social interaction by talking with the chickens as she would her peers. She had found a non-judgmental outlet to express herself.

Hilarie and I loved each of our three children as they were, each with their unique strengths, and we were mindful to observe the lessons they could teach us, as well as those we could teach them. They each kept me looking up from my chores; kept me from parceling time as packages on a conveyor belt, a slave to my smart phone's schedule. I was thankful for childrens' brilliantly naïve view of their surroundings.

Ten

Anticipating our winter livestock housing needs, in mid-June I constructed a hoop house for our expanded laying flock. About 60 layer chicks were ready to leave the brooders, and they would be housed in the hoop house until fully grown. By that time, fall would be upon us and the older layer chickens currently out on pasture could be brought into the hoop house and combined with the new layer chickens. Combining flocks could be a tricky thing; larger birds would chase and peck the younger birds. The "pecking order" is a real thing; it is the way chickens establish their social order. Combining them when they were all about the same size would minimize conflict.

Hoop houses are normally used to extend the vegetable growing season, but they are also a great way to house chickens for the winter. Ours was to be 12 feet wide by 32 feet long, with metal hoops constructed from salvaged chain link fence rails (I got a deal on them from a local fencing company), bent into a curve on a home-built jig, spaced every 4 feet. The hoops were anchored by first driving a slightly larger pipe about two feet into the ground at each end of the hoop, sliding the hoop ends into the pipes, and fastening them with Tek screws. The hoops were joined together by two tiers of 2"x8" pressure treated boards at their bottoms. These skirt boards would also hold in the chickens' bedding. A single straight pipe was screwed to each hoop at its apex, joining them all together. The end walls were constructed of 2"x3" lumber and 3/8" plywood, with a salvaged storm door my parents gave us and adjustable wooden shutters for ventilation. The structure was covered with translucent greenhouse plastic. Six foot tall chicken wire fastened to the inside of the hoops kept the chickens from pecking holes in the plastic.

We expected the hoop house's interior to be beneficial to the health and egg production of our layers. Egg production is related to day length and light brightness. The hoop house would maximize the chickens' access to daylight, and provide warmth via passive solar heating.

In order to start with a level bottom line for all the hoops, Dad and I set level stretched string lines outlining the structure. Then we located and drove the ground pipes with a sledgehammer, until all their tops were even with the string lines. Driving the pipes was hard work in the rocky soil, and of course it was a hot and humid day. After driving the ground pipes, we set the hoops in place, and that ended the first day's work.

The next morning I set the skirt boards. Because the ground beneath the hoop house sloped, I needed to do some trenching with a pick and shovel to keep the skirt boards at or below ground level; there couldn't be any gaps beneath them, or else we'd be chasing pullets around the yard.

Holes dug around our farm were archeological expeditions. I have always loved to dig; I tried to dig tunnels when I was a kid and spent high school summers backfilling railroad tie breakwaters on Cayuga Lake with a wheelbarrow and shovel. And I had dug a lot in the last fifteen years since we moved back to the farm: excavated the old house's stone foundations by hand to rebuild them, dug probably 100 post holes for fences, porches, and outbuildings, removed topsoil for stone walks, etc.

Over 150 years, our ancestors had built, deposited, and abandoned all manner of things on our land. Our lawns were filled with buried treasure and old foundations. At least I considered it treasure. Every object had a story; was a family relic. I kept everything I found and stored it all in one of our sheds.

I found some short pieces of chain, a few broken pieces of blue glazed china, and a harrow tooth while I was digging trenches for the hoop house skirt boards; pretty typical stuff. I brought it to the shed to add to the collection. But I had found much more interesting stuff in previous archeological digs...

The mysterious wheel: The first order of business when we moved back to the farm was to install a septic system and a well. We hired a contractor to dig holes for and install the piping, tank, and leach field for the septic system, and another contractor to drill the well. While digging a four foot deep trench for water piping near the old horse chestnut tree behind the house, the excavation contractor found a large and very rusty round object, about five feet in diameter. It was buried deep. It could have been a wheel for some old tractor, but it was covered with rows of rivets and was solid. It looked like a giant clutch plate, or a giant electricity-generating dynamo from an old Frankenstein movie. It was buried again when the contractor backfilled the trenches. There it still lies below our lawn, an early industrial mystery.

The mechanic's dump: We tore down an old carriage house and put a house trailer on its floor slab as a temporary home when we started renovating the farmhouse. One day, Hilarie decided to plant tulip bulbs at the edge of the slab to one side of where the carriage house's sliding door had once been. She pushed the shovel into the ground; obstacle one inch down. She tried an adjacent spot: same thing. Working along a six inch by four foot strip, after an hour's work, she had a trench 4" deep and a pile of black, greasy soil filled with rusty spark plugs, pieces of chain, nuts, bolts, and baling wire. I remember when people used to change the oil in tractors by taking the oil pan plug out and letting the oil drain across the driveway. This had been an area where motor oil was dumped, and I remembered a weedy patch filled with scrap here from when I was a kid. Hilarie did not share my affection for digging and was angry at the results of her project. But she planted the bulbs anyway, and filled the trench with the same oily dirt and junk she had dug out. Amazingly, the tulips sprouted just fine (I also remember my Great Grandmother's hollyhocks growing in this same spot amid the weeds, probably at the same time oil was being dumped here).

The sub-slab dump: Years later, after we moved into the renovated house, we sold the house trailer and had the carriage house floor slab broken up and removed. As the backhoe picked up large pieces of the slab, its base material was revealed: large round stones about six inches in diameter, probably picked from the back fields. I could imagine the stones being hauled by horse and cart to the site of the carriage house and thrown off into the pile we now saw uncovered for the first time in 100 years. These stones were piled six inches to a foot deep under the slab. And scattered among the stones was household garbage circa 1911, the date scratched on one corner of the slab. There were deep blue and white enameled pots (always with a rusty hole somewhere in the bottom), and bottles. And more bottles. And more bottles. Somewhere along the line, one or more of my ancestors must have become addicted to "patent medicine," which was mostly alcohol. Most of the small bottles were the same, cast with the name of a long-gone local pharmacy. We found about thirty of them scattered within the stones, and most were unbroken. I could imagine some great grandfather or long lost uncle stopping at each unloading of the stone cart to sip two or three bottles of the "medicine." Could it have been his way of getting around the Temperance movement popular just before Prohibition?

The reaper burial ground: There was an old McCormick reaper lurking in the weeds behind the equipment shed when I was a kid. These devices were horse drawn and used to mechanically cut and bundle grain crops. They saved a lot of work; before their invention grains were cut with a scythe and shocked (bundled) by hand. The bundles were subsequently hand threshed of their seeds in the barn, until mechanical threshers were developed. The reaper in the weeds was very old; it was half rotted into the ground forty years ago when I last remember seeing it. It was made mostly of wood, with cast iron fittings used to join the wooden pieces, and some steel for the gear drives, sickle bar cutters and wheel rims (the wheel spokes were wood). A few years ago, I cut down some large box elder trees that were leaning dangerously over the pole barn, cut their stumps below ground level, and tilled and regraded the area. Just below the lawn's surface was the resting place of the old reaper. One by one the tiller's teeth found its pieces: wheel rims, cast iron attachment pieces, square head bolts, pieces of angle iron, chains, gears, wheel hubs. I think I have a complete reaper in my archeological artifact shed; it just needs the wooden pieces to join all the metal parts together.

Other discoveries: On an adjacent side of the carriage house from the oil dump site, I found about 100 pounds of cylindrical lead battery cores. Grandpa had sold and recharged 24 volt battery systems, mainly for lighting use, before rural areas had electricity. The batteries were green glass square jars; cubes about one foot on a side, filled with acid, and the cathode and anode (+ and -) hung from their sides. Grandpa used one of these old battery jars to ferment raisin wine when I was a kid.

When our solar electricity panels were installed, the contractor dug a trench from the pole-mounted panel arrays in the back field to the electrical panel in the garage. On the way, he hit one stone foundation after another. He had to loop all the way around these foundations to bury the electrical conduits. Whoops, I had known about these...they were originally built as side-by-side, long, narrow rabbit houses, and later used to store firewood.

When I was young, the farm had more than a dozen outbuildings, including two large bank barns and the two story carriage house. Other structures included an equipment shed, a coal house, a pig pen, a half dozen rabbit and poultry houses, an outhouse (of course!), and a blacksmith shop (for shoeing horses and other metal repairs) with a front room holding the winter sleigh. By the time Hil and I moved back home, all was gone, rotted into the ground or torn down before they collapsed, as we had done with the carriage house. How I wish these structures were still standing!

When we were tilling the lawn for reseeding after we finished the house, a man with a metal detector stopped and asked if he could look for buried objects. Oddly, found nothing but some pieces of an old aluminum TV antenna and an 1890's dime. We let him keep the dime.

*   *   *

Once the skirt boards were installed, I needed only to build the 2"x3" stud and 3/8" plywood end walls and cover it with greenhouse plastic, which I had ordered custom-cut online. Constructing the hoop house kept pulling me back into the past, as I thought about all the structures previously built on the farm. It happened that the hoop house was located beside the former location of the main bank barn. When the ground became dry during summer droughts, the outlines of the barn foundations seemed to rise out of the ground. I don't know whether this was caused by the shrinkage of the clay soil or the dead grass revealing more of the ground contours.

Beside the hoop house, between it and the barn foundations, was a mysterious circle I had wondered about for years. It was definitely the outline of a foundation, but the circular shape was puzzling. Old wooden silos sometimes were circular, but this foundation was only about five feet in diameter; seemingly too small for a silo and too big for a hand-dug well. And none of the photos of the barn I had, which dated back to the 1890's, showed a silo. Dad couldn't remember anything ever standing there. I wondered whether this foundation could pre-date the construction of the barns in the 1880's. After all, our land had been settled around 1800. What was here before? Anything?

Old maps showed there were many things around

our farm of which no trace remained. I often imagined my ancestors' intertwining relationship with this place over the course of 200 years, starting with my Great Great Great Great Grandfather, Hendrick Miller.

Hendrick (Henry) Miller was born in Pennsylvania in 1784. He married Catharine Lern in 1802, and the two made their way, in the winter by sleigh, to Lansing in 1804. The trip took three weeks. They brought a heifer calf, and building and farming tools. The route from Pennsylvania to Lansing, New York was the frontier of settlement in those days, and they stopped at cabins along the way, obtaining food and rest at each stop as was the custom for hospitality back then.

Henry was an enterprising man. Upon their arrival he built a cabin, and in subsequent years he acquired land, piece by piece. By 1814 he owned 380 acres, mostly on Revolutionary War Lot 74 (land was used to pay war veterans). Our farm occupies 45 of those original 380 acres. Eventually he replaced the cabin with a large house, and it still stands as the home of a neighboring farmer up the hill from us. On the four corners adjacent to our property, he built and operated a distillery, cider mill, cabinet shop, and grocery store. It was a little town of sorts. The barn which contained the cider mill was torn down five years ago, and the store (which had become a home), just two years ago.

Henry died in 1837, and Catharine in 1843. She bore ten children over the course of 16 (!) years. One of those children was Frederick Miller, born in 1805, my Great Great Great Grandfather. Frederick married Elvira Ingersoll, and I imagine the two settled on a portion of the land that had belonged to his father, as it was the custom for families to give their male children pieces of the farm upon their marriage. Chances are, this land included our farm, because Frederick would, in turn, deed some of his land to his son, who built our house.

Frederick and Elvira had five children, one named Irving Miller, born in 1835. Irving was my Great Great Grandfather. Irving married Esther Loomis in 1869 (a late marriage at 34 years of age!). They had only one child: Clara Miller, who was my Great Grandmother. She was born in 1880. I share my birthday with her: October third. I also bear a striking resemblance to her, and feel a connection to her that is difficult to explain.

I am sure that Irving and Esther Miller built the house we live in, probably in 1883 (when we renovated the house, we found "June 28th, 1883" painted on some boards behind a chimney). They owned our current farm, plus some adjacent property containing farmland and a "hired man's house," which burned in 2004. I wonder why Irving married so late and why he and Esther had just one daughter. He seemed ambitious; he built all the original barns and outbuildings I have written of, and our beautiful Greek Revival farmhouse. Photos from the turn of the century show the farm to be well kept. Irving died in 1921 (at the age of 86; long life was in his lineage), and Esther preceding him, in 1912; both here on the farm.

Their daughter Clara (my Great Grandmother) married a Swedish immigrant named Peter Larson in 1900. She was twenty years old, he was thirty-four. Peter was my Great Grandfather. Clara, with and without Peter, would be the driving personality on our farm for the next seventy years; she would see it through its transition from "Miller" to "Larson," and would preserve it in its original form until her death.

My Great Grandmother was a liberated woman on the front edge of the suffragette movement, although we have no records of her being a registered member. In her early years, she was not one to be stuck on the farm. She worked on the Ithaca-Auburn railroad for a while in her youth, walking up and down train car aisles selling candy, cigarettes, and other sundries. It was a mile walk to get to the train station down the hill from the farm. I wonder what the neighbors thought of this; it certainly didn't seem the norm for a young girl raised on a farm. I have also heard she traveled with a "patent medicine show." (translation: snake oil salesman) Scandalous!

Somewhere during her travels she met and married immigrant Peter. Their marriage lasted long enough to bear one son, Dwight, in 1901. The family story about their separation was that one day Peter arrived home to find Clara "sitting on the lap" of another man (we can guess the translation of that). That was the end of their marriage. Peter moved to Ithaca and worked for Cornell University until his death in 1961 (another long life at 95). He is my and my father's namesake, but exited the family picture after only a few years, long before either of us was born.

Clara lived her entire life on the farm, and had a reputation for making the finest butter around. When we renovated the house, we found a dozen lard butter-crock seals in the dirt-floored basement. Lard was poured on top of the butter to seal and preserve it. The lard discs had become so hard they were used as stepping stones in the basement. Clara also raised rabbits, and sold cooked, deboned, and canned rabbit meat. The farm had an orchard, gardens, and chickens in addition to milking cows and horses. Self sufficiency was the order of the day.

Clara seemed to do just fine managing the farm and raising her son Dwight on her own. I never knew her, but my father says she was a stern woman. She must have been strong to carry on for seventy years (albeit with the help of several male friends I think).

Although her butter and other sales provided for her and her son and kept the farm out of debt, there was little money for upkeep. The buildings that were pristine under her father Irving's attention gradually fell into disrepair, and by the time of her death, the roofs were leaking on many of them, including the house. The fortunes of the small family farm in general changed greatly during her oversight from 1900 to 1970. Farms specialized, and took on debt to grow. Her farm remained a deteriorating time capsule of life in the late 1800's. I am thankful and proud of her for that. For whatever reason, she moved against the grain, just as I have a tendency to do so.

Great Grandmother Clara died when I was 18 months old. It was her son Dwight, my Grandfather, who I bonded with and respect so much. As I have written, he carried the old ways from his mother down to me. But he was no more perfect than any of us.

Dwight relied heavily on his mother for validation; he lived with her most of his life. He also was fond of alcohol and loved conversation. His career off the farm consisted of driving a truck for a local lumber mill. In 1935 he married a neighbor, Ester Keeney, who had previously borne one daughter fathered by another man without marriage. They had an on-again off-again relationship over the following decades, producing five more children, one of which is my father, Peter. Their family arrangements were always changing. They lived together and separately on and off the farm, in a nearby house they purchased, and on Ester's siblings' large family farm. Their children: my father, aunts, and uncles spent long periods living alternately with their parents together or separately, or with other relatives.

My parents, Peter and Jacqueline, were married in 1965 and moved back to the farm soon after I was born in 1968. They cut a small square off the farm adjacent to the old farmhouse and built a house of their own. This is where I grew up, spending much of my time next door with my grandfather until his death in 1977. After my grandfather died the house was empty until Hilarie and I returned in 1996. The barns came down one by one between 1977 and 1996.

Dad made a go of beef and pig farming for a while after Ggrandpa died. He built a large pole barn, cleared out the hedgerows, and improved the drainage of the land. We grew our own crops to feed the livestock. Our freezer was always well-stocked with meat, and he never had a problem selling what he grew, but Dad had a full time job. He decided to quit farming while I was in college, and began leasing the land to neighboring crop farmers.

I sat under the walnut tree by the partially constructed hoop house feeling the privilege of continuing a long lineage few others can share in this age of disposability and mobility. A great responsibility came with this privilege: to hold this farm for the family's future generations, to instill in our children Hilarie's and my love of place, and to teach them to sense the energy of our farm I feel so strongly. The journeys of my ancestors were almost visible in my lingering eyes.

Eleven

Though they were on pasture, our meat chickens still consumed a lot of feed. The birds' growth rate was too fast to subsist on greens and occasional bugs. About 30% of their diet came from the pasture and 70% from feed: mostly a mixture of cracked corn, soybeans, and oats. Still, the 30% pasture portion, along with the sunlight and fresh air they grew in, made a world of difference in their meat's nutritional qualities and flavor. During the height of the chickens' growth, around week six, a pen of 50 meat chickens would consume 115 pounds of feed per week. Plus we had pigs, turkeys, and laying chickens to feed, all on pasture and all requiring supplemental nutrition.

There are few domesticated animals that can survive solely on pasture. There are some breeds of cattle that can, and also some breeds of sheep, goats, and pigs. There used to be many more. Subsistence solely on pasture has been gradually bred out of many breeds in favor of supplementary feed to boost growth rates. For some, especially cattle and other ruminants, this practice of grain supplementation actually can sicken the animal. But it is used anyway.

Every week during the summer, I drove our pickup truck to the local feed mill, about ten minutes' drive from the farm, usually right after morning chores. Our farm was still too small for the mill to deliver in bulk, and we had no large feed bins to store weeks' worth of feed in. I had read cracked grains quickly decline in nutritional quality, and felt feeding the freshest feed possible was one of those details that could make our products just a little better than others'. So it was a weekly trip, and I would return with 50 and 100 pound bags of feed, 500 to 1,000 pounds total, which I opened and poured into galvanized steel trash cans with watertight lids out on the pasture where the birds were, and near the pig pasture. Portable infrastructure in action!

I had come to the feed mill ever since I was a little kid, riding with Grandpa. I don't remember the specifics of his transactions there. Grandpa had a small hammer mill in the main barn on the farm, and he ground his own corn into feed. The hammer mill was driven by a long belt that ran through an opening in the barn wall, out to the belt pulley on his 1940's Farmall H tractor. There were slatted corn cribs around the outside of the barn into which husked ears of corn were loaded in the Fall. The ears were fed into the hammer mill from the corn cribs, and the feed was stored in several small bunkers in the corner of the barn. Each bunker had removable wooden planks across its front. As the bunker was gradually emptied, one plank after another was removed from the front. Each bunker was lined with old license plates and flattened tin cans; futile attempts to keep rodents out of the feed. Grinding was a noisy, dusty operation. Grandpa and I would be coughing, half deaf, and completely white with dust at the end of the day. I remember the dogs chasing vermin out of the corn cribs as the piles got smaller and smaller and the resident rats and mice, with no place left to hide, bolted.

Dad tore down the barn containing the hammer mill. When he grew corn, we brought wagonloads to the mill to be ground. Unloading at the mill was easy if you had a dump truck; not easy with a wagon. The unloading area had a pit beneath it into which you dumped your crop. The pit had angled sides and an auger at the bottom to bring the material into the mill. We had to shovel our corn off the wagon and into the pit.

The feed mill was near the center of a small town, really just four corners with a gas station, diner, mechanic's garage and the auction house I attended on Friday evenings. My weekly summer routine was always the same: I walked into the office building and said hello to the ladies working there. The office walls were covered with wood paneling circa 1975 and it smelled of cat litter. It took me a surprising number of visits to make the connection between the importance of keeping cats and having a feed mill. The ladies in the office were always very nice, "Hi

Pete, how are the chickens doing?" They knew my business, and sometimes knew what I needed without my having to tell them, "500 pounds of range broiler, 200 pounds of swine ration, 100 pounds of game bird starter," etc. They wrote the order on an old-fashioned receipt machine, the kind loaded with a roll of duplicate carbon paper, and a lever on the side they would pull to dispense the two copies of the receipt: one for me and one for the office, which was stabbed for safe keeping onto a vertical nail attached to a piece of wood on the counter. There was not a computer in sight; this place hadn't changed in my lifetime. After I paid, they called the order out to the guys in the mill via an intercom.

I walked back to my truck in the parking lot across the street and pulled it around to the loading dock, which was on the side of the main mill building directly behind and attached to the office. Sometimes I had to wait a few minutes while a delivery truck was loaded. I never minded the wait; this place was so full of memories, and the mill buildings were so interesting; there were always new details waiting to be noticed.

The main buildings: the mill, the storage barn directly behind it, and the railroad loading station across the street, were over 120 years old. The mill itself was clearly the center of the business. It was a large wooden building encasing the old milling and grain elevator machinery, which poked out of its roof and sides as if it had outgrown its original skin. Up on the roof, one large pipe exited straight up. At its top it joined a half dozen pipes which angled back downward, and entered the roof at various points along the building. This was how feed components were stored. Each component (corn, oats, etc), one at a time, was carried upward in small buckets attached to an endless belt. This happened in the large vertical pipe. The buckets dumped their load, one by one, when they reached the top. A set of diverters was turned so that whatever component was being stored would than fall down one of the angled pipes into its assigned bin inside the mill building. When it came time to mix the feed, valves on the bottom of each of the bins were opened to meter out specific weights of each component, according to the required feed recipe. The feed flowed out the bottoms of the storage bins by gravity, to the mixing operation on the ground level of the mill. Grain elevator and milling technology had changed little in the past century; many parts of the main milling apparatus were original to the operation. It was powered by electrical motors now, but I imagine it must have originally been powered by a steam engine or a large gasoline/distillate engine.

Directly behind the mill was the storage barn, another large wooden building which looked just like the old barns on many farms. Once feed was milled, it was trucked over to this building, 50 feet behind the mill. A wagon entered the bottom level of the barn via a ramp, and then the feed it carried was loaded into one of the dozen or so storage bays above. I do not know how the feed was moved upward into the bins. One time I asked one of the guys who worked at the mill and he did not know either. It had been a long time since this building had been used for feed; now it was for miscellaneous storage.

Once the feed was in the bins on the upper level of the barn, it could be loaded onto customers' trucks or wagons via a row of wooden chutes that exited the barn by a series of keyhole shaped openings all along one side of the barn at loading dock height. Each chute dispensed a different type of feed, and the keyhole shape of the opening had something to do with the mechanism for raising and lowering its hopper door (Once again the guys at the mill weren't sure of the specifics).

The original location of the mill must have been partially determined by its proximity to the local rail line, as the third prominent original building was a train loading depot, across the road from the other two main buildings. I could imagine crops being unloaded from train cars here, and cars leaving loaded with freshly ground grain. No remnant of the rail line remained. This building had long ago lost its original use, and it was now used as another storage building.

Aside from the three original buildings, four or five more wood and concrete block storage buildings had been built over the years. The mill, as a whole, was a large part of the small town; containing the tallest structure and occupying the most land.

I loved being able to buy our grain at the mill. Although the mill did not produce organic feed (GMO free, pesticide free, etc.), it ground locally grown grain, employed local people, and formed one heart of a local town. I loved its history: its old buildings, the train station, the way it preserved an essential part of early American rural life. Fifty years ago there was a mill like this in almost every town. There was even one in the middle of downtown Ithaca. The milling process and the ethic embodied in it was an important part of the story we told our customers about our chicken.

How we obtained our feed really did reflect an ethic. We could have gone to the local chain store to purchase 50 pound bags of feed, could probably even have negotiated a better price than we were paying the mill (by the way, our feed expenditures were far and away the largest expense of our farm). But this place where we bought our feed was *meaningful*.

At the mill, we knew where our feed came from; we knew some local farmer had sold it to them. We knew there was less diesel fuel embodied "in" the feed; that is, it had been trucked a minimal distance. We could see what was in our feed; could recognize the yellow pieces of cracked corn, the hulls of the oats, and the brown powder of the ground soybeans. The chain store feed was an unrecognizable brown crumble or pellet; anything could be in there.

We supported the local economy with our purchases at the mill. It employed about 15 people from the local community. Our dollars wound up in the pockets of local farmers and community members. We also supported the life of the mill's community with our business. What would this community be without its mill? What would take its place if it ever left? Physically it would be a town with one of its hearts cut out. It would still have its diner, gas station, etc., but the loss of the mill's historic architecture would remove a large piece of the community's unique identity. Small towns such as this one had little to fall back on when a major part like the mill was removed; they became just another blur passing the car window on the way to someplace else.

Despite all this, the mills that used to exist in almost every town are going the way of the local butcher. There were a dozen mills within twenty minutes' drive when I was a kid, now there are just three. The other mills are gone, flattened; another sucking void in local economies, the victims of government subsidized fuel prices and the centralization made economical by that. I naively hoped our local mill could avoid these forces.

In November I received a letter from the mill owners. Prominent on the letterhead were the logos of two national companies. The mill had been sold; the present owners were retiring. Local milling would cease; feed would be trucked in from several "regional" facilities. The letter assured me that quality service would continue and the special feed blends the local mill had developed would continue to be offered; just ground somewhere else.

Why had this happened? Didn't other people see the mill as I saw it? Couldn't they recognize its importance to the community's identity, its history, the memories it embodied? Couldn't they see the physical, ugly void its demolition would leave? Things I cared so passionately about: preserving the unique energies of place and community, had long been dominated by the inhuman and often cruel forces of economics. I knew this from my old life in architecture.

Every place on the Earth has its own, unique energies. When I was an architect, I learned how to sense these energies, define them, and put them into terms others could understand. Healthy, living places were made, or most often grew, via working with, not against, their underlying energies. I think people used to sense these energies of place more than they do now, and used to value them more than they do now. The loss of this sense had increasingly allowed economics to dictate the qualities of places, and resulted in the creation of more and more "dead" places: shopping strips, placeless housing subdivisions, whole centers of communities blown out for corner drug stores and parking lots.

Lest you think I'm off in the clouds with this sort of talk, here are some practical examples. I used to design schools, which are often one of the centers of a community. School buildings embody many literal forms of energies. The energy expended in their making is the fuel used to dig foundations, the energy used to create concrete, steel, bricks, and glass. The energy expended in their upkeep is fuel used to heat and electricity to cool, the energy used to make replacement materials for those that wore out; carpets, windows, furnishings, etc.

School buildings also embody many non-literal forms of energy. Every school building project starts with the investment of energy by those who advocate for its construction: parents, teachers, school boards. As a center of the community, every school building also houses the energies of all that has occurred within their walls: the memories of all the children that studied there, the events in the building that brought the community together; sports, school plays, lunches, fundraisers.

The place the school building occupies contains its own energy, there before the building was built and (hopefully) strengthened by the construction of the building. It could have been a forest teeming with life, a city lot which once held businesses central to the community, an older school filled with memories but demolished because of its age or its size. But most often, it was the energies of nature that most dominated a place: the sun's path, the direction the wind blew, the plants and animals that had once thrived there, how water flowed across it.

It took no magic to see these energies. And it took no special powers of persuasion to convince others of their importance. If I was talking to an audience with a pragmatic character, I focused on the literal investment of energy in the school building. If I had a passionate audience, I focused on the power of preserving memory and the energies of community identity. Usually, my audience spanned the full range between these poles, and my message of working with a place's energy resounded with each audience member on their own frequency. If I performed my job correctly, I could convince my audience that preserving and enhancing a place's unique energies was more important than most, if not all, economic considerations. After all, quality of place was deeply related to quality of life, it talked to the core of our being and our emotions. I could bet on emotion beating economic consideration any day of the week. I had learned that personally via my own passion for and connection to the place in which I lived. My health was tied to the health of the farm.

I felt recognizing and working with the power of place was about more than just architecture. Certainly, it translated to farming. I thought some of society's ills were related to people's loss of connection to place; that becoming a part of a place provided a necessary nurturing of the soul, and that living in "placeless places," such as nondescript housing subdivisions, was contributing to this illness.

The mistake my old profession made was in ignoring the energy of the places in which we build. Or more correctly, in having forgotten to observe; instead favoring modern architecture's more academic, cold, analysis of place. This was part and parcel of industrialism, and following right behind it was our allowing economic considerations to take the place of true quality of life considerations. I was passionate about working to change that.

Now I was seeing the same forces at work on the old mill: an ignorance, an insensitivity, to the energy of place, and the irreversible damage that would be done to the community. I could not blame any one person for this, but I did blame the collective ambivalence of our society for allowing such things to happen.

There were other powers at work here. The local mill was part of a bygone era of low energy systems. Feed is heavy to transport, and local mills existed to minimize transport distances and time. This was especially true when draft animals were used and during the early days of the internal combustion engine. Mills were located near rail lines, taking advantage of their low energy transportation systems. Now this expenditure of energy was cheap; economics said it made sense to truck feed from Albany, four hours away. No one with any common sense could say this made sense, but economics did; fields full of crops lay a mile away from the mill! Fuel had become artificially cheap, subsidized by the government via tax breaks and grants for exploration, through its securing of overseas sources, and by not accounting for the environmental costs its burning produced, or by the costs of the changeover in technology that would need to occur as its availability declined.

In December, Hilarie and I went to the mill to make our first purchase since its ownership transition. Five ladies worked in the office previously, now Nancy was the only one there, along with a young man wearing a hat and shirt bearing the logo of the new feed company. We often assume things about people based on their appearance. I had received my fair share of others' preconceptions because of my long hair and beard; now I subjected his appearance to my own prejudice. Here was a man I would have a hard time trusting, with his short hair, neutral appearance, and corporate apparel. This attitude was reinforced by his attempt to sell me layer feed for my heritage turkeys. Didn't this guy know anything about appropriate protein and calcium percentages? I was no feed expert, but it appeared I knew more than this guy. And, it appeared this guy would soon be the only one in the office.

Hilarie and I climbed into my truck to go get the feed I had ordered. The man in the office had directed me to a concrete block warehouse with an arched roof on the other side of the road, behind the old train station. Walking inside, I was met by one of the young men who used to load my feed from the mill loading dock last summer. The warehouse was filled with 50 pound bags of feed in plastic bags, on pallets. I had lots of questions for him.

He informed me he was the last employee left; the only person who would be loading feed from now on. His job was to man this one warehouse, where all the feed would be kept, and to load customers' vehicles from its loading dock. The warehouse reminded me of the one at the end of "Raiders of the Lost Ark," gloomy and lonely. Periodically new pallets of feed would arrive from Albany. Feed could still be bought in bulk, augered off the truck into bulk tanks at the farm, but still, the feed would be ground in Albany. All the other buildings on the property would be torn down; the mill, the old storage barn, the train station. I guessed this was to reduce building maintenance and property taxes. Everything I loved about this place would be gone forever, replaced by a man in an office wearing the logoed shirt of his corporate masters. "It sucks," said the man in the warehouse, I'm sure feeling more helpless at this turn than I did. How could so many farmers protest big government while at the same time allowing themselves to become the subjects of big, inhuman corporations?

I left the warehouse angry and sad. Another piece of Grandpa's world was gone and could never be replaced. I would not do business with this place. Next year I would have to find some large feed wagons and transition to bulk feed delivery from one of the two other mills, both about a half hour away. Who knows how long those mills will remain in business?

Twelve

When I was working in Syracuse, I drove 25,000 miles per year. I bought a new car every four years and filled up the gas tank twice a week; all on the company's dime. I traveled to make presentations to clients and at conferences: I drove all around New York State and flew to many large cities across the US. I stayed in nice hotels and ate at great restaurants. This seemed like a great gig.

Once my six month leave started, I rarely left home. I liked that just fine. I replaced my 50 mile commute with a weekly trip to the feed mill or Agway. I replaced fine dining in Manhattan with Saturday evenings out with Hilarie while a sitter watched the kids, running errands, and eating at one of the restaurants in Ithaca. We were always home by 7:00 to put the kids to bed. I'd be surprised if I drove more than 1,500 miles in those six months.

The traveling life consisted of destinations and the

blur between them; disconnected places. I had a work life and a home life separated by a blur. I did not feel part of a community in either place. I loved where I lived but had few connections to the surrounding community.

When I started my leave of absence I wanted to connect with the local community. I was vague about this; is there any such thing as "community," in the singular sense? Each of us belongs to many community subsets, and their circles of influence and common interests cross and re-cross like the circles in a Venn diagram. The auctions were a first step; the auction house felt like a community gathering. I saw the regulars week after week and got to know them, some of whom I had known before and were even relatives of mine. That was a confluence of two or three separate communities.

Building the farm connected me with another community: getting to know the guys at the local lumber mill, feed mill, and Agway. The farm supply community.

Learning about, reconnecting with, and meeting my neighbors placed me in yet another community: the farmer next door I had grown up with, the long lost high school friends that lived just down the road, the large farming families neighboring ours who I had known all my life and lost connection with in my placeless existence between Syracuse and home. This community connected me with my newest and closest friend, Keith Thomson.

When I began vending at the two farmers markets, the population of my community exploded. All of a sudden I was meeting dozens of other farmers who shared many of the same ideals I did. The same held true for customers. These were special bonds. These were the folks I socialized with outside of business, starting with Keith: potlucks and dinners at friends' houses, guys' nights out for dinner and beers.

Finally, I reconnected with community in a political sense, starting with Keith's wife, Sarah Thomson, who introduced me to a circle of people who saw the issues facing our local community similar to the way I did. I dipped my toe in the water with this community, lending support and a hand if needed, but hesitant to become involved much with contentious things, still healing from my prior life.

Wonderful things started to happen when my community circles grew enough to begin recursing; when an acquaintance of an acquaintance looped back with an automatic connection to me. People I met for the first time who said, "Oh yes, I heard about your farm and how good your chicken is from so-and-so. What a wonderful life change for you!" An automatic bond!

I learned that connecting with community was dependent on feeling part of my place; the farm. When I commuted, I didn't care about my community; when I wasn't working I was at home, busy with projects, with little time for community interaction. When I took leave, I spent almost all my time at home, and gradually began to reach out to connect with community. It seemed natural. Now I had time. My place, my farm and family, had to be connected to community for my family's, my place's, and my own health. It had only taken me twenty years to realize that; twenty years with a go-it-alone attitude.

The farm was my anchor to the community; it gave my family its place within the whole. And wow, did I have some stories to tell about our connection to this place! I'd been building them up, silent to the community, for the last 15 years. The history of my ancestors was one story, and there was an equally important story about what happened in the years following Hilarie's and my return home.

Hilarie and I were married in Syracuse in the fall of 1995. Even before we were married, we started making plans to move back home and renovate the old farmhouse. In the summer of '95 we photographed the house, and I took measurements and made architectural drawings of the existing building. That summer, with Dad's help, we also demolished the carriage house to provide a place for the temporary house trailer. We salvaged what wood we could out of the carriage house: its oak timber framing, maple floor beams and roof rafters, and 12 inch wide hemlock siding.

We bought a used house trailer for $4,500 using cash we received at our wedding. In the summer of 1996, we parked the house trailer on the carriage house slab and had the septic system, well, and electrical service installed. There was a 20 foot deep stone-lined dug well near the old house that provided great tasting water, but such wells were no longer allowed because of water contamination caused by fertilizer runoff and other chemicals. Instead, we wound up with a 40 foot deep well that produced water smelling of sulphur. Hmmpff.

The trailer was a dilapidated old thing, built in 1974 with wood paneled walls that visibly bowed when the wind blew, and a furnace that always gave out in the middle of the coldest nights. On those nights we had to leave the faucets dripping to keep the water lines underneath the trailer from freezing. I joked that having to live in the old trailer would force us to renovate the house as quickly as possible. In hindsight, it was the most efficient housing we could have chosen: three years later when we moved into the house, I sold the trailer for $3,500. We had spent just $1,000 for three years' housing.

The trailer was a gem compared to the condition of the old farmhouse. The house, seen from above, was laid out with two wings forming a "T," and a third wing that came off the rear of the "T." The first two wings were 1½ stories (the second story's rooms had sloping "pan" shaped ceilings) with a fieldstone-walled, dirt-floored basement. Downstairs, these wings contained a formal parlor, informal living room, pantry, and a small bedroom. Upstairs there were two large bedrooms. The third wing was one story, and contained a kitchen, small dining area, and mudroom. There was a short crawlspace under this wing, and a stone and concrete six foot by six foot cistern, accessible by a trap door in the kitchen floor (relatives told me Grandpa hid whiskey bottles during Prohibition by floating them in the cistern). All the house's downspouts led to pipes that brought rainwater to the cistern. The cistern provided soft water for washing dishes via a hand pump up to the kitchen sink. The house had four brick chimneys: three at each gable end of the "T," and one for the wood cooking stove in the kitchen wing. Altogether the house was less than 2,000 square feet, excluding the basement; quite small.

All the roofs of the house, except for one half of one roof over the north wing (which had asphalt shingles on it), were still covered with wood shakes (shingles). All had leaked since Grandpa's death in 1977. The second floor had rotted so badly that the floorboards crumbled away when stepped on; we had to lay planks across the floor joists if we wanted to cross a room. A fallen limb from the horse chestnut tree behind the house had partially collapsed the kitchen wing. The front porch had almost completely rotted away. We could stand on the first floor, look up through the second floor, and see sky through the holes in the roof. The house had minimal electricity; most rooms had one light with an outlet in the fixture. There was no plumbing except for a toilet Grandpa had added off the kitchen, with a pipe that led to a small covered concrete block box buried in the lawn nearby. On the (very small) positive side, the house was an 1880's time capsule; almost nothing had been changed since it was built.

People thought we were crazy to renovate it instead of tearing it down. These opinions had a reverse effect on me; they hardened my resolve to finish the job. I was beginning to form contrarian opinions about the role of economics in decision-making processes. This place was a part of me; had been ever since my childhood days with Grandpa. No economics argument could trump the loss of this place.

Hilarie was a saint in agreeing to take on this project with me. We were looking at years of hard, dirty work, and the sacrifice of all our free time. I did not have very much construction experience, and we were running on faith that we would learn how to do things as we went. Still she believed in the project and in me.

In the summer of '96, after getting settled into the house trailer, we began work on the house. The kitchen wing was too far gone, so we tore it down and salvaged what lumber we could. Up in its rafters, above the kitchen ceiling, we found the "attic stock" from the house's original construction: extra pieces of mouldings and wide planks. There were many custom mouldings on the house: at the porch columns, the roof's eaves, the window frames, and the baseboards. This stock would help us to replicate some of the shapes.

Next, we stripped all the wood lathe and plaster from the walls and ceilings. This was the messiest task of the whole renovation. Much of the plaster had already loosened because of the roof leaks, and came down with a swipe of the shovel. The lathe came off with a crowbar and hammer. All the plaster, including that on the ceiling, was covered by many layers of wallpaper. Once we had pulled everything down and it was piled on the floor, we shoveled it into garbage cans or out the window into a wagon below. The work was dusty. Hilarie and I wore masks that helped a little, but at the end of each day's work we still coughed for hours. This work took us a few weeks in all. It turned out that the lathe and plaster had been bracing the house upright more than I thought; at the end of the work, I could stand on the second floor and swing myself back and forth, and the whole house would move with me. After finding that out, I hurriedly installed 2"x4" diagonal bracing on the inside of all the walls!

Before the work on the upper stories could continue any further, the foundations and wood sills needed to be fixed. The foundations were made of random sizes of fieldstone, uncut and laid 1 ½ feet thick. Simple lime and sand mortar had been used to lay the stones, and over the years the mortar had deteriorated to the point where I could pull out by hand just about any stone in the top three feet of the walls. These top feet were the areas where the walls were most subject to freeze-thaw cycles and alternations of wet and dry soil. Below this, the walls were solid and just needed repointing: the removal of old mortar and insertion of new mortar at the stones' surface joints, inside the basement. On top of the foundation walls were the mudsills, seven inch by seven inch chestnut timbers, used for the species' rot resistance. Unfortunately, even their resistance had its limits and they were mostly all rotted, due, probably, in large part to the roof leaks. This rot extended about six inches up almost every wall stud.

I hadn't the means to jack the whole house up to repair the foundation walls and replace the mudsills, so I came up with a way to work around the perimeter of the house, 12 feet at a time. First I nailed

16 foot long 2"x12" boards to every wall stud (the wall studs were spaced one foot apart instead of the customary 16 inches), on both the inside and the outside of the wall. The house was balloon framed, which meant that a single 2x4 stud ran all the way from the top of the mudsill to the bottom of the roof. Then I shored up the two studs on each end of the 2x12's, making sure they had firm support on the foundation wall. Next I removed the mudsill and stud bottoms in the 12 foot span supported by the 2x12's.

This gave me access to a 12 foot length of the foundation wall, which I tore down, stone by stone, until I reached solid wall. As I tore the wall apart I had to excavate about two feet of earth around the outside of the house with a shovel. I would place the foundation stones I removed in reverse order on the lawn; rebuilding the wall upside-down so I could remember which stone went where. Even so, they rarely fit back together they way they had come apart!

Next I mixed mortar and rebuilt the wall. Old stone walls were built to accommodate some movement and water migration, and the lime mortar used in them had self-healing properties: if a crack formed and water ran through it, some of the lime in the mortar would dissolve and re-harden at the surface of the crack. In keeping with this idea, I used a primarily lime and sand mixture for the replacement mortar, adding a small amount of Portland cement to increase its strength and shorten its cure time.

Slowly, I rebuilt the section of stone wall. Getting the stones to line up and form a level top was one of the hardest parts. I ran string lines along the walls to keep them level and straight. Once the stonework was finished, I built a new section of mudsill out of four pressure treated 2"x8"s laid on edge and nailed together, with the boards' ends staggered so the next section of wall could be locked together with the current one. Finally, I jacked the 2"x12" braces up to remove any settlement that had occurred from the rotting of the old mudsill, sistered new pieces of wood connecting the cut off 2"x4" studs with the new mudsill, and removed the 2"x12" braces.

I spent the remainder of the summer and fall of '96 repairing the foundation, piece by piece. At this pace, I thought it would take ten years to finish the renovation. Sometimes I got discouraged. When this happened, I would walk around to a piece of wall I had finished and would admire my work; take pride in the stonemason and carpenter I was becoming. The project as a whole was overwhelming; I had to think about it one piece at a time.

I could have saved a lot of time by replacing the bad sections of stone wall with concrete blocks, but I was determined the outside of the house should look exactly as it had when it was first built. Passion trumped economics and pragmatism once again.

Once the foundations were repaired, I began replacing the roofs. The original roofs were wood shakes nailed to rough-cut boards. The boards hadn't been squared on their sides; they still held the shape of the trees from which they had been cut. The south wing was completely rotted: roof, rafters, and ceiling joists. The entire structure from the top of the walls upward would need to be replaced. The brick chimneys would need to come down too. They were built on the top of small closets in the bedrooms, a dangerous structural condition to begin with. And the bricks crumbled apart when touched. They had formed an important part of the appearance of the original house, but I could think of no way to replace them.

I reroofed the north wing first, removing the shakes and planks and putting a new plywood covering on the old rafters. One of the slowest parts of this job was the replacement of the rotted wood trim at the eaves of the roof. It had a complex moulding profile and was made of three separate, overlapping boards. Using a router, I cut new boards with approximately the same profile. After these were installed, I finished the north wing roof with asphalt shingles. How good it felt to have half the house dry again!

The south wing was a bigger job. I tore the whole roof structure off, down to the tops of the walls. Then I built a new structure to replace it, and a new shingle roof on top of that. By mid-summer '97 the house was dry for the first time in twenty years.

Still, the work remaining was daunting. The pine clapboard siding, trim, and windows all needed to be replaced. Working wall by wall all the way around the exterior of the house, I removed all the siding from the wall studs and nailed up plywood sheathing covered with Tyvek. I removed the windows and reframed the window openings in preparation for wood replacement windows. This was complete by the time the weather was beginning to get cold.

During the winter of '97/'98 I worked inside, replacing the first and second floors. All the floors and all the floor joists, except the second floor in the north wing, were rotten. I started with the first floor, framing it with new joists and plywood. Finally an entire floor I could walk on! The second floor was trickier, because it affected the structural integrity of the house. The fact that the house was balloon framed, with single wall studs that ran all the way from the mudsills to the bottom of the roof, helped maintain its integrity while I replaced the second floor of the south wing. I did the work carefully in eight foot long sections, removing and replacing the floor joists and installing the plywood flooring section by section.

When the weather broke in the spring of '98, I began installing the house's new wood exterior over the plywood sheathing and Tyvek I had installed the previous year. This was my first try at finish carpentry; I really needed to pay attention to detail here. As the house was in the Greek Revival style, it had wood columns on its corners, complex mouldings around just about everything, and an ornate front porch.

I would do this work side after side, starting with the east side of the house, which faced the road. First I installed the new windows, then the wood trim and mouldings around the windows, then the corner columns and mouldings, and finally the cedar clapboards. I'll never forget the first window I trimmed! It was beautiful. Just as the house had been in old pictures! I was proud of myself.

Re-siding the house took most of the next year. This was my favorite part; seeing the house emerge as it had originally looked. Neighbors stopped by to compliment my work. During the winter of '98/'99 I finished the drawings for the interior reconfiguration of the house. I had kept the exterior true to the original, but the interior needed to be modified, mainly to include bathrooms and a larger kitchen/dining wing, which needed to be constructed new from the ground up.

Hilarie and I decided the interior work was too much for us to do ourselves. There were too many specialized trades (plumbing, electrical, etc.) and we were tired of living in the trailer. We had a contractor price the work, including constructing the kitchen wing. Until now we hadn't accumulated any debt with the house's renovation, and we did not want to take on a large, long mortgage. We settled on hiring the contractor to perform the minimum amount of work it would take to make the house livable: insulation, drywall, plumbing, electricity, heating, and a temporary kitchen in the existing pantry. The floors would remain plywood for now and the new kitchen wing could wait a few years. For these compromises, our mortgage was reduced to fifteen years and we paid it off in eleven.

The contractor started in the spring of '99 and finished the work in the fall. Hilarie and I moved into the house and rattled around in its spaciousness, compared to the old trailer.

Renovating the family home was the most meaningful thing I had accomplished in my life. I

153

regret nothing about the entire process. Those who had shaken their heads at my foolishness now complimented the quality of the job. It helped define who I am today. It gave me the self confidence to take on just about any project, not only in construction. I could figure out anything I put my mind to.

Hilarie and I settled into our new home as I continued construction activities. I installed new oak and maple floors throughout the house. The wood came from trees Dad and I cut down near the house. Dad and I had both swung from a rope hung from one of the oak tree's limbs when we were children. All the wood was cut into boards onsite with a portable mill.

In 2003 and 2004, I built a three bay garage with a second floor where the carriage house originally stood. We planted gardens, built picket fences, and gradually furnished the house.

In 2002, our first daughter, Cora was born. In 2006, our second daughter, Grace was born. The house we once rattled around in now seemed small. It was time to build the kitchen wing.

The kitchen wing would almost double the size of the house, from 1,500 square feet to 2,600 square feet. It would be one story high, with a mudroom, kitchen, pantry, and dining room on the first floor and a TV room in the finished basement. For this project, I decided to do all the work myself, except the excavation and pouring of the concrete foundations (didn't have the expensive equipment) and the finishing of the drywall (would have taken me forever!).

In the spring of 2006, the foundations contractor started work. By the fall, I had the exterior of the addition completed. Dad helped me put up the wood framing. I started work on the plumbing, electrical, and heating systems. As the winter of 2006/2007 progressed, I completed the plumbing and electrical rough-in and finished the heating system, and installed insulation and drywall. Hanging the drywall was especially memorable. I could not do this work alone; the sheets of drywall were too heavy. Dad and his two brothers, Mike and Brownie, came over to help for the weekend. I can't ever remember the four of us spending this much time together, and the memory means a lot to me. We had fun and worked hard; by the end of the weekend most of the drywall on both floors was hung.

I hired a professional drywall man from down the road who moonlighted on weekends to finish the drywall. Small world; he had worked on some of my jobs in Syracuse. He was done in three weekends. We moved into the first floor in the spring of 2007, and into the basement TV room in December 2007.

For the interior of the addition, I focused on reusing materials we had accumulated in demolishing parts of the house and the carriage house. These had been stacked in the pole barn over the years. The large opening between the kitchen and the dining room was framed with oak timbers salvaged from the carriage house, as was a structural post in the TV room. The wall behind the TV was covered with chestnut floorboards salvaged from the first floor of the house. The cathedral ceiling in the dining room had exposed roof framing, again salvaged from the carriage house timbers. The wall separating the addition from the original house was covered with hemlock siding salvaged from the carriage house. Below this wall the stones from the original foundation wall were left exposed, with the stair to the basement running alongside them. Hanging in the middle of the hemlock wall was a crosscut slab from the trunk of the giant horse chestnut tree my Great Grandmother had planted when she was young. The stairs leading from the dining room down to the basement TV room were made with oak from the tree my Dad and I had swung from as children.

In the spring of 2008, we hired a landscape contractor to finish the lawns and walkways around the addition. When they were finished, we were DONE. After 13 years, we had realized our dream of renovating the house which meant so much to my family's history, and had constructed an addition during which I had learned almost every skill necessary in home building, at the same time incorporating meaningful materials from our family's history into the structure. We couldn't imagine ever living anywhere else.

Right around that time, in 2008, I was in the middle of my first major career change at the firm, turning my focus from general practice to green design. In hindsight, I think I was looking for another purpose as meaningful as the one I had discovered while renovating the house, and green design seemed to fit the bill. This started me down the path that would eventually lead to my leaving the firm, and the merging of reactivating the family farm (originating from work on the house) with celebrating the energy of place (originating from my place and refined in my architectural work).

Thirteen

We are born our life laid above us as a great tree, our choices a journey up the tree to one of the multitude of buds at the tips of the treetop. We are given the potential for so many sorts of greatness, a particular route to a particular bud and its particular genius. Each tree is our own only, shared with no one and twining its branches with so many others' trees surrounding.

Our choices trend from grand to nuance. Complete halves, thirds, quarters of the tree put behind us by the choices of our youth, so filled with energy and optimism, and so ill-equipped to see the implications of the branches taken. Conformity and convention, the simpler climb of the tree, creeps in with an icy numbness, lulling us to a quiet and nameless existence. We sleepily while the years away while our own greatness lays a branch away, separated from ours by cardinally naive decisions early in life and now knees too weak to jump the span. Jump!

A very few of us are weighted toward greatness on trees bowed with fertile buds. They are assigned a grace of potential and a terrible weight of expected genius, known only to each bearer. Each chosen reveals that grace and weight in different proportion. Some arch beautifully upward with a knowing rightness of path, their peace and brilliance a blinding and enviable light. Others sink under its weighty obligation, their life a forced march to achieve their potential.

And for some sad number of us, no matter our heart, no matter our longing, none of the buds are fertile, and we spend our life scrambling against this, retracing our steps to make new paths, only to end our hunt again and again at the same frustration: mediocrity. We flash a raging despair at our lot; a knowing we are making our best, but it is a flimsy of the greats who shine through us as blinding lights crowding humanity's roar for attention.

We may wonder at, be beaten by, the hand that judges the value of our life. There is, most certainly, an extant reckoning that cares not of one's subjective fulfillment. No matter some's security, they ask for the judgment of that hand. This sickness chases them into every place of refuge.

I hope the wisest know many seeming mediocrities as quiet greatness in disguise, for this is mine and most's true path to inner peace. To be happily ordinary is feat of genius of itself, a loving and quiet embrace of life.

-"Chance Great Mediocrity" December 2012

*   *   *

My subconscious is a pretty reliable prognosticator. It knew my career in architecture was moving toward its end years before it came to pass; knew it as Hilarie and I we were finishing the house in 2008. I was destined to celebrate the oneness of a simple life on the farm and its accompanying philosophical reflections. As I said before, it just took me twenty years to consciously realize this.

In 2008 I made a decision to focus my career on sustainable (green) design. General architectural practice had worn me out; I had lost interest in climbing the same hills, project after project. Sustainable design was, and still is, a rapidly changing part of architecture. It was exciting to surf the waves of rapid change, and it was noble work to get involved with. It was a complete flip for me: while the house renovation focused on hands-on, hands-dirty, physical activity, my approach to sustainable design was dominated by theoretical and abstract explorations; refreshing new territory to learn.

As usual, I moved against the grain; contrary to the direction in which most of the building industry was moving. I wanted to talk about the end-game; what a sustainable future could look like, and what relationships were necessary to create that future: human to human relationships, human to natural world relationships, and humans' relationships to the technology they created. I asked, "Did a break need to occur somewhere along the line? Was one of our current relationships fundamentally flawed?" I knew the answer was yes; that we had never properly coexisted with nature. Although we were a part of nature, it was always treated as some "other" thing, apart from us, to be used. This was the root of our present environmental ills. It extended all the way back to the origin of Western scientific thought and its Cartesian view of the universe. Characterizing nature as a collection of "resources" went right to the heart of this. Unless you were a pure Transactionalist, would you characterize any other person solely as a "resource?" Nature needed to be treated as a subject, like another person, instead of an object to be used and abused. Eastern philosophy and Native American tradition gave me a good start for my investigation; they had always seen the world in this way.

Meanwhile, the sustainable design field as a whole was focusing on creating incrementally more natural resource efficient buildings. This was a very technical thing. It involved a lot of sophisticated software to model building resource use, and research to find more environmentally friendly energy systems and materials. I did not want to minimize the importance of this sort of work. In fact, I saw passive solar design, first made popular during the 1970's energy crisis, as a topic that united this technical focus with the more philosophical things I was working on. Passive solar design is about our relationship with nature; how our buildings interact with the natural world via the paths of the sun and wind, and local climate.

I wanted to make my mark in sustainable design; leave a trail of original thinking that would be remembered by others. I guess at first I wanted to become famous, as some other architects were, for doing original work in sustainability. I traveled, lectured, and wrote. But as the world wore on me and I realized how psychologically ill-equipped I was in the role of a public renegade, those hopes of fame left. Late in my career I expressed poetically, in the essay that leads this chapter, the satisfaction of the realization I was meant to live a life that celebrated the ordinary.

One such ordinary activity that spoke of one of the most powerful concepts I explored during these years was the simple act of cutting and burning firewood to heat our house.

Hilarie and I originally heated our home with a central boiler. In 2008, I installed a clean-burning wood stove; one which re-burns its exhaust gasses and cannot be dampered down to a dirty, smoldering fire. This was a natural decision for me. Burning firewood for heat had a long tradition in my family. Throughout my childhood, I helped Grandpa and Dad cut firewood. Some of my favorite memories surrounded this; resting with Grandpa in the woods, talking while he smoked his pipe, and feeling good after a hard day's work cutting firewood with Dad.

To fund our heating transition, I sold about twenty sugar maple trees in our woods for lumber. A father and son team cut down the trees, cut the straight logs out of their lower portions, hauled the logs to the mill, and left the branching treetops in the woods. I used some of the money I received for the logs to purchase the wood stove, and the treetops lying in the woods provided about four winters' worth of heat after they were cut into firewood. Given our efficient wood stove and the amount of trees on our land, it was a sustainable way to heat our home. Wood heat is also carbon-neutral, meaning it adds no new carbon to the earth's carbon cycle, unlike coal or oil which is

163

added to the cycle from below the Earth's surface. The increase in atmospheric carbon from such sources is thought to be one of the primary causes of global climate change.

We located the stove in the front room of our house. Heating with wood created a major change in the house's interior environment. I remembered this from when I was a kid; how Grandpa sat in the 80 degree stove room to reduce pain from his arthritis, and how cold our family was on winter mornings before Dad reloaded the stove.

Our boiler had kept the entire house at a uniform temperature whatever the weather. We paid little attention to whether the boiler was on or off, and only noticed when something went wrong and the temperature fell below the norm. When we installed the woodstove, we had a central system mindset. We wanted to maintain a uniform temperature. What a lot of work that was! Our stove was designed to only burn hot and clean; there was little we could do to adjust it. So with the goal of maintaining a somewhat even temperature, our day included a repeating routine of rekindling the stove and letting it burn down, including getting up in the middle of the night to do so.

We gradually grew out of our central system mindset to accept more temperature variability. Maintaining an even temperature was too much work! On cold days when the outside temperature was below twenty degrees, we burned the stove all day and the house gradually got warmer from morning to evening. We reloaded it before bed and let it burn to a few embers overnight. The house cooled overnight and the warming cycle started again the next day. Sweater in the morning, shorts in the evening.

On warmer days, thirty degrees and above, we either waited until lunchtime to start the stove, or burned a load in the morning and a load in the evening.

This may sound like an awful inconvenience, but it wasn't; the extra work was offset by several satisfying rewards. It gave us a feeling of connectedness to nature. The wood stove put us more in tune with the weather and the forecast. We planned ahead for the temperature swings of the coming day and night. We learned to appreciate temperature variability; that our house was 90 degrees in the stove room and 65 degrees in the upstairs bedrooms. When I came inside from working in the cold I sat in the 90 degree stove room to quickly warm up, with my cold toes facing the fire. I read or wrote in the dining room, halfway along the stove's temperature gradient through the house; 70 to 75 degrees and comfortable for sitting. When we went to bed in the evening we piled on the blankets and enjoyed the coolness of the 60 to 65 degree bedrooms. Throughout the day we could move to where we were most comfortable, often based on task.

And, I liked being self-sufficient. I felt good about being responsible for our heating's entire supply chain; forest to stove and all the accompanying labor.

I have met other folks who heated with wood and saw it as a lot of work with no reward other than the money saved. We saw it differently. Our wood stove

165

was a constant connection to nature, and a mechanism to see the value of one of nature's primary characteristics: variability.

I thought about my experience with the woodstove and how its lessons could be translated into architecture and sustainable design. This became one of the centerpieces of my philosophy, a topic that came to be called "control and variability."

We prefer order, and exert control to create order. Our order has evolved to be different than that of nature. Wild nature is not random and is characterized by variability; it is subject to another order to which we are not accustomed but once were. Relaxing the control of our order and accepting the variability of nature's order reconnects us with it and allows us to learn how to work in concert with it.

Previously I presented a simple equation:

$$\text{Control} = \text{Energy} = \text{Homogeneity} = \text{Waste}$$

Following this equation, the less control we exert over our environment, the less energy we expend and the more variable our environment becomes. This applies to the temperature inside our house, the amount of weeds in our lawn, how clean we keep our house; anything.

This equation also works the other way: If we want the temperature of our house to be constant year round, if we want a weed-free lawn (or cornfield), if we want an immaculate house, or if we want every piece of wood siding on the outside of our house to be exactly the same (homogenous), then we must exert more control and expend more energy.

Our relationship with Nature is fundamentally flawed; we treat it as an object rather than a subject. But we can never see it as a subject or another personality without releasing some of our control of it, thereby allowing its inherent variability to present itself and reveal nature's own order lying beneath. We need to perceive this order as its personality in the course of our mutual interaction. Much of this personality has been masked by industrial technology's domination of nature with its own order: monocropped fields; stone, wood, and other natural building materials cut all the same size and selected for uniformity of color, texture and grain.

We need to release some of our control simply to save energy and other resources! Lawns don't need to be mowed every week (I crusaded against the environmental impact and wasted energy of lawns, only half tongue-in-cheek). Buildings can fluctuate more in temperature: open a window or put on a sweater! More variability can be embraced in construction materials; it creates a richness long missing from many of the cold modern buildings I had worked on earlier in my career.

The variability topic relates to the passage of time in two ways. Variability exists *across multiple points at the same time* and *over time*. Variability across multiple points at the same time allows us to choose which condition of that variability to favor and occupy; like moving between the rooms of the house in the wood stove example. Another example of this is nature

167

builds things according to a highly variable blueprint. We can look at ten frogs, ten trees, ten people, and no two will be the same, although we will recognize each as "frog," "tree," or "person."

Variability over time is the temperature of a single room over the course of a day. In nature, things rarely stay in stasis for long. Temperatures are fluctuating, living things are growing or declining, elements such as water are changing phases in cycles; ice to water to vapor over and over again.

We can use these models of variability to change our design value sets. We expend a lot of energy to make buildings and other things look eternally new: repainting wood, replacing worn carpeting, and so on. If we embrace variability over time, we can design buildings to age gracefully, using materials like unfinished wood and stone that require minimal maintenance and the expenditure of less energy.

We also expend a lot of energy to make buildings and other things with pieces that are all the same. What if we made blueprints as nature does, and allowed more variation in acceptable materials? Again, energy would be saved and waste reduced.

Often folks would ask me for various analogies of the way I thought we should relate to nature. If we had to change our relationship, what sort of a relationship should it be? Certainly we needed to release some of our control, but we couldn't give it all up, living like cavemen, completely subject to nature's will. I responded we should think of our relationship as we would a healthy marriage. We have always been wed to nature, but for too long we have dominated the relationship. Healthy marriages are about deeply knowing the other, about give and take, about understanding how one's health is essential to the well-being of the other.

We have to *reconcile* our troubled marriage with nature. Reconciliation is a path of respect and cooperation. If we relax the control of our order to learn and subsequently value the complexity and variability of nature's order, then we can learn to remake our order to be complementary to nature's order.

This marriage is something unique to each of us; something we have to come to our own terms with, just as the successful union of any two people is unique, based on their personalities. Relationships begin within each of us and with emotion. No one can give us a flow chart for creating a healthy, mutually beneficial, and fulfilling marriage. The same is true for our relationship to nature. We can come to agree on attitude, benefits, qualities, and ideals, and yet the emotion and dynamic of every person's relationship is different.

I worked on control and variability, and other concepts following my "relationships" view of sustainability, until my departure from the firm. The profession of architecture as a whole seemed obtuse about the whole thing. Some folks just wanted to be told what to do, instead of being challenged to define their own healthy relationship with nature. Some had no relationship with nature; their only interface with it was the walk from their car into work (or wherever) and back again. They were ambivalent about any deeper relationship. But most of all, modern design sensibilities were so intertwined with industrialism and its domination of nature, that, try as I might, I could not untangle them.

Other architects saw sustainability as a technological thing; felt that new building systems like higher efficiency equipment, better insulation, and renewable energy from the sun and wind were the answer. How convenient such solutions would not force them to be introspective of their design values. I think the "technological fix" is also the dominant public view. I disagreed.

We have all the technology we need to live sustainably; in fact to heal the damage we've done to the world and to each other. To be successful, we need to understand the issue is really one of our relationships with each other and nature. The solution lies well beyond the narrow views of energy consumption, pollution, and natural resource depletion. There are more than enough food and natural resources available for us; for the whole planet. The real issue is that these resources are grossly unequally distributed among the world's population, and that we waste too many resources on rampant materialism, war, and the gross over-use of energy because of its artificially low cost.

Sometimes I thought this could be reduced to even simpler terms: Just find a place on Earth and care for it; love it as a part of yourself; and wed your health to its health.

I didn't realize these solutions until late in my architectural career, possibly not until after I had left it. Once I realized them, I lost respect for the wandering machinations of the profession, the over-complication it brought to simple things, and the way I had been a part of that.

The farm was a much more direct way to practice the philosophy I had developed. Living a life of Great Mediocrity, with the ability to focus on and refine an uncomplicated and healthy relationship with nature, was my answer.

Fourteen

Early August's summer apex arrived and our farm was yielding its fruits. Literally so: this was the best central New York apple growing season in recent memory; even our four year old trees had a half dozen large apples each. I plucked one off a tree and bit into it on my way out to the pasture to do Saturday morning chores. Delicious.

There is a wonderful feeling in providing for yourself; be it growing your own food, harvesting your own solar electricity, or even simply cooking your own meals. The beginning of August was the time of overabundance: summer squash, tomatoes, pole beans, salad greens, swiss chard, and beets grown in a shady corner of the garden. The elderberries were ripening for fall wine making. The tree frogs were beginning to keen high in the walnut trees. One afternoon the kids and I found one at the base of one of the trees and held it, examining its round suction cup toes and delicate bright green body. I loved the herbal fragrance of the bee balm in bloom and watching the hummingbirds' visits to them and the trumpet vines in the pergola over the garden gate.

Just about all our meals were made with ingredients either from our farm or from nearby farms: quiches made with our eggs and summer squash, pasta sauces with our fresh tomatoes, pesto from the herb garden, our barbecued chicken, barbecued organic hamburgers from Schefflers' up the road, Keith's perfect salad greens, tomato and lettuce sandwiches, on and on.

We were thrifty with the food we grew because of our personal investment in it. Leftovers were never thrown away. Barbecued chicken scraps became chicken burritos and sandwiches; soups and quiches were made with whatever ingredients were on hand or coming from the garden. Little was left: vegetable trimmings, stale bread, and greens which had bolted were fed to the chickens and pigs as treats. Our compost pile didn't see much fresh material anymore.

Even as we enjoyed August's bounty, we were starting to prepare for the long winter. Hilarie was canning and freezing vegetables, and we had bought a giant new chest freezer. We wanted to ensure our customers a continuous supply of frozen pastured chicken through the seven month long part of the year when it was normally not available; when the pastures' growth slowed in October, winter covered them with snow, and their grasses lay dormant until April. I had four pasture boxes of 50 chickens each running the pasture, their ages staggered so they would be ready for weekly butchering. Starting that August, we would grow 350 more chickens by the end of the season in November; over half the chickens of our first year. 200 would go into the freezers pre-sold to the customers of our chicken CSA.

There were also two batches of turkeys on the pasture. These were the industry standard broad-breasted white and bronze breeds (our heritage Bourbon Red turkeys would arrive later and be grown in a coop through the winter). One group had hatched at the end of May, the other at the end of July. The turkeys took longer to grow than the meat chickens, at 16 vs. 8 weeks. We had a slightly different process for raising them as well. Turkeys spent five weeks in the heated brooder before moving out to pasture, then spent another five weeks in a standard chicken pasture box - fifteen to a box - moved to fresh pasture every day. When they outgrew the box at ten weeks, we moved them to a stationary covered roost surrounded by portable electric net fencing, powered by a solar fence charger. This whole setup moved once every week or two, depending on the condition of the pasture. Turkeys are voracious on pasture, and we would start their appetite for greens while they were in the brooder, pulling pasture grasses and salad greens from the garden to feed them every day. The turkeys' electric net fence was only four feet tall. It was meant to keep predators out more than keep the turkeys in. The turkeys could fly over the fence but rarely did. When they did, they never went far; they did not want to be separated from their flock. We just walked up to the escaped bird, picked it up, and put it back in the fenced area.

We had found that the electric fence was not perfect at keeping predators out, in fact none of our fences were. One morning, I found a four week old dead meat chicken just inside the chicken wire side of the pasture box, apparently bled to death through a small slash in its neck. There was very little blood on the ground though. Having run more than 200 chickens over the pasture already, and having lost none to predators, this came as a shock. A few times I had seen where animals had tried to dig tunnels under the pasture box walls, but none had been successful in the one night a pasture box was in a particular location. The occurrence didn't repeat over the next few nights, and I chalked it up to a random predator.

Soon after that, we tried moving a flock of turkeys directly from the brooder into the electric net fencing setup. Hauling a pasture box with just 15 turkeys in it was a lot of work. A few days after moving the turkeys onto pasture, I found two dead one morning, laying by the fence. The killer had the same M.O. as the earlier chicken killing: bleeding the neck cleanly and leaving the carcass. I moved the remaining turkeys into a pasture box. The next morning one more was dead against the chicken wire side of the box; again, same M.O.

Losing a chicken was one thing, losing a turkey was completely another. Folks were already pre-purchasing turkeys, and each turkey represented a significant investment and income for the farm. A large turkey could sell for $75 or more. I talked to other farmers at the market and learned these killings fit the description of a weasel. I heard horror stories of weasels that got into chicken coops and bled 30 chickens in one night. Weasels could reach through the one inch wide hexagons in chicken wire fences, grab a bird by the neck and suck its blood out.

The weasel had only killed one chicken out of 200 on the pasture, but had killed three turkeys from a single box of fifteen. The reason was the chickens usually slept huddled together in the back corner of the box, which had corrugated sheet metal walls, while the turkeys usually slept right against the chicken wire walls in the front half of the box. The turkeys had done the same thing in their electric net fenced pasture. The weasel could reach the turkeys but not the chickens.

The weasel never bothered the older turkeys in the other electric fenced enclosure. They had taken to sleeping on top of their shelter, and were unreachable to the weasel. The weasel also seemed to prefer small prey. So I set about "weasel-proofing" the one pasture box containing the younger turkeys. I screwed plywood over the chicken wire on the sides of the box, and cut a piece of plywood to cover the front of the box at night. Every evening I covered the front side with the plywood and braced it with a feed bucket, then removed it in the morning. I also bought a clever deterrent online: two solar powered sets of red LED "eyes," which blinked all night long. The product advertising said they warded away predators by appearing as another, larger predator in the darkness. I mounted them to pieces of pipe and moved them every day with the cluster of pasture boxes, pushing the pipes into the ground. We never lost another bird on the pasture to predators after that.

We did lose two layer chickens in one night, and had a third seriously mangled, in the hoop house less than 100 yards from our house. The hoop house had large ventilation openings covered with chicken wire in its end walls. Each opening had plywood covers that could be adjusted up or down. The chickens took to roosting on the top edge of the plywood covers, and somehow the weasel scaled the smooth plywood wall and grabbed three chickens. I started raising the ventilation covers at night so the chickens could not roost on them and this fixed the problem. The chicken that had been mangled lost a large portion of the skin on its neck, and spent a month in a hospital pen. But that was the end of the weasel's midnight buffets.

Anyone living in the country knows, with livestock or without, that there are destructive animals that need to be dealt with. Some are predators and some are not. Have-a-heart cages may work in the suburbs, but we in the country know the vacuum that nature abhors is more quickly filled if the woodchuck is driven a mile down the road and dropped off vs. receiving a bullet to the head. Our weasel was an immediate concern, but the effects of other pests grew over the course of years, damaging buildings and gardens.

Ever since we moved back to the farm, our woodchuck population climbed year after year. So did the red squirrels. The woodchucks ate our garden crops and made a mess of our lawn and the inside of the pole barn with the holes they dug, the red squirrels chewed holes in the eaves of the barns and piled walnuts in every empty box and flower pot. Dad was perpetually at war with the red squirrels. It seemed like a bad zombie movie; for every one he shot with the .22 caliber rifle, five more would appear.

While Dad went after the squirrels, I had a long-standing vendetta against the woodchucks, formed ever since they had decimated a particularly excellent crop of broccoli Hilarie had grown. But unlike Dad, I was a lousy shot with the .22, and couldn't even catch them in have-a-heart traps. So last year I had purchased four leg traps from a company in Alabama. The leg traps were a choice of last resort; a way to catch animals that caused suffering as their leg was held in the trap until they were shot. Hole after hole, den after den, I exterminated all the woodchucks around the pole barn, under the stone walls at the edges of the yard, and in the hill in the little cherry woods in the pasture. I set two leg traps at the two exits to a woodchuck's warren, walked out with the .22 in the morning and evening, and shot the woodchucks caught in the traps. Then I moved the traps to the next sets of holes. That summer I killed 40 woodchucks. My second cousin and neighbor Bradley Keeney worked the hedgerows and fields in a half mile radius around our property, and killed about 400 woodchucks during the same year. The following year I saw only two woodchucks around the yard, but in future years I'm sure I'll see more. Like I said, nature abhors a vacuum. It's a never ending job.

Rabbits are also pests, eating our garden greens, but are much easier to take care of. If I walked out in the morning and saw a rabbit in the lawn, the rabbit froze and I walked back into the mudroom to get the .410 shotgun. The complex working of the rabbit's mind is, "as long as I don't move, they can't see me." So I walked back out with the .410 and shot the rabbit where I had left it. One evening I shot six rabbits in the backyard, one after the other, walking in and out of the mudroom for fresh ammo, following just this process.

There was no pride in these activities, beyond that of knowing our buildings and our crops were protected. One could be proud of their expertise in managing country pests, but the act of killing, at least for me, was simply a necessary thing. It felt akin to the morality of butchering chickens; a part of the cycle of life. Each creature held a karma I was careful not to take lightly.

On this Saturday morning in early August, I had no worries about woodchucks, red squirrels, rabbits, or weasels...I was doing chores, munching on a fresh picked apple and trying not to get chicken poop on it (occupational hazard). Saturdays were the farmers market in the park in Homer. The dewy, cool morning with bright blue skies above heralded a sunny day and I was looking forward to the positive vibe of the market. After I finished the chores I went into the house to say good morning to the kids and eat breakfast, then loaded the big cooler full of chicken into the bed of the truck. All the other market supplies: tent, table, signs, etc. stayed loaded in the back seat of the truck through the market season. I got the cash box from the kitchen cabinet, and headed off to make the 9am market opening.

I pulled the loaded truck up to the curb at the park in the center of town and unloaded my wares. This had become routine; in ten minutes my stand was set up and my truck was parked on the other side of the street, allowing customers easy access to the parking spaces adjacent to the market. I was ready fifteen minutes ahead of the opening bell as usual, and sat back in my lawn chair, sipping coffee and watching the rest of the market get ready for business.

The markets brought a rhythm to my life. After I started my leave of absence, the days of the week began to fade. My activities didn't change much from one day to the next over a seven day cycle; chores were done every day, special projects were too. But once I started selling at our two markets, the days of the week took on a rhythm: Sunday, Monday and Tuesday were project days, Wednesday was butchering day, Thursday was packaging and labeling chickens and other preparations for market, and Friday and Saturday were market days.

The location of the Homer market is truly beautiful. Homer is a small town with an old time Main Street; brick row buildings butted side to side with businesses on the lower floors and offices or apartments above, interspersed with large old churches, homes, and a public library. The park the market is located in had been deeded as public land in 1804, in remembrance of Revolutionary War veterans.

181

Its sidewalks are lined with mature trees, and it is surrounded by the buildings of Main Street on one side, and old homes, large old churches, and a public school on the other sides. An octagonal bandstand is located in the middle of the park. Our market tents lined the sidewalk in the park along Main Street, in the shade of maple trees.

Here at the height of market season there were about 25 vendors; 25 interesting characters who all had great stories to tell about their lives and their trades. There was the hydroponics farm located on a couple acres just out of town, started by two young men just out of college with lots of positive energy. There was Eileen Scheffler, my neighbor with the organic beef and dairy farm. There was the incredibly energetic Laura, who had three young children and still managed a business painting watercolors and selling produce. There was the couple from New Jersey who made and sold soap: Bob and Nancy. They were living a double life with day jobs in Jersey and weekends in Ithaca and Homer, renting an apartment nearby and looking to buy a house to complete their transition to upstate New York. And there was one of my favorite characters, the tattooed Punk Rock Michelle, who sold custom made hula hoops (weren't hula hoops a hippie thing, should she have been selling spiked dog collars instead?) I remember our first conversation.

Pete: "Why do they call you Punk Rock Michelle?"
Punk Rock Michelle: "Because I like punk rock."
Pete: "Oh."
By chance, my booth was at the center of the

market; at the intersection of the sidewalk along Main Street and one that ran perpendicular to it, to a brick church at the back of the park. This was rare luck for a vendor's first year, as everyone jockeyed for the best locations. I got to listen to a free concert every market day. I was right across the sidewalk from the empty spot where different musicians played each week, usually folk, roots, bluegrass; the homegrown mix of local music unique to the culture of the markets.

Markets were about conversation as much as sales. Markets were the way to connect with new customers, and to network with other vendors. This relied on getting to know each other, in forming a personal connection with the people who purchased our products. When I was an architect, the trade shows I attended served a similar purpose, but these were harder work as we had to be "on" for the entire show. This was exhausting because being "on" was not really being yourself; it was being an amped-up, more friendly and talkative version of your real self, and you were always searching for a connection to the potential client you were talking to.

Conversation at the farmers market was genuine, and connections with potential customers centered around food were easy to make. They liked good food; we grew good food. There you go! From here we could talk about our farming ethic, how they had become conscious of the importance of local food, my life change from architecture, and general issues surrounding our communities.

My next door booth neighbor at the Homer market was Tomi, who made and sold granola. She and I shared a small open space at the corner where our booths met, facing the musicians' spot. This we dubbed our "porch." We would pull our chairs here and watch the musicians play, and we would talk. Tomi was a pastor who took temporary positions when local churches were between permanent pastors. Her husband was the pastor of the big brick church to which our sidewalk led. Tomi brought me one of her breakfast smoothies every week, and I enjoyed sitting with her and taking in the market scene.

Back down the sidewalk heading toward the church was Daniel's booth. In my opinion, Daniel got the award for the most beautiful produce arrangement every week. He made his displays out of salvaged barn wood, and his "Two Spruce Farm" sign was hand painted on undyed denim. Daniel was in his mid- to late-twenties, had a degree in English, but had chosen another path. Currently he was an apprentice at a sheep dairy that used draft animals - horses and mules - for power. As payment for his apprenticeship, the farm owners gave him a place to live and a small piece of land to grow vegetables on, which he sold at market.

Daniel was one of a growing group of bright young people who saw farming as a meaningful and noble life. I was always encouraged when I met people like Daniel. Working with one's hands, mastering a craft – any craft, not only farming – had long received less respect than it deserved, and resulted in the movement of many intelligent young people away from the trades. This was changing. I had realized its

184

importance midway through my career, but Daniel had been bright enough to see it right at the start of his.

The sheep dairy was Daniel's second apprenticeship. In the fall he and his girlfriend would be moving to a permaculture farm in Vermont for another apprenticeship. Eventually Daniel planned on buying his own farm. The experiences of his apprenticeships would help ensure he was successful when he did so.

Daniel had read about my work as an architect, and was interested in sustainable design. He had thought about attending the Yestermorrow design/build school in Vermont before he started his path toward farming. He liked to talk about philosophy, and understood the abstraction of my former work focusing on relationships in architecture, so we had many interesting talks over the course of the summer.

That Saturday Daniel came over to my booth and we started talking about the economics of local food. This topic had been bugging me for some time and I wanted his thoughtful opinions on it.

In Homer, but not so much at the Ithaca market, there were two groups of customers: the "looky-lou's" and the "locavores." The looky-lou's came to the market for a nice morning stroll, and might purchase a pastry or a bag of greens as an impulse buy. The locavores did a significant share of their grocery shopping at the market. The Homer market offered almost everything required for a week's meals: pork, chicken, beef, vegetables, grains, herbs and spices. Its great selection was not being taken advantage of as well as I thought it should be, despite the excellent marketing efforts of the market organizers.

Homer's crowd had more looky-lou's than Ithaca's, and this troubled me. It seemed a simple case of demographics: food was more expensive at the farmers market, and Ithaca was more affluent than Homer. I asked Daniel, was it right that healthy food be accessible only to the upper income classes? Of course it was not we agreed, but what could be done? It was way beyond us to answer this question; was something we as a society were struggling with. There were certainly many people who either hadn't the means to afford good, healthy, and locally grown food, or did not have access to it where they lived. But Daniel and I also recognized that many people had the financial means to eat this food, but did not for a number of other reasons:

Education: Some people do not know the differences between healthy, locally grown food and mass produced industrial food. Food education, like many things, often follows class lines, with wealthier people being more educated than poorer people. There are still people who aren't familiar with the growing and slaughtering practices of concentrated animal feedlot operations (CAFO's), increasingly resistant strains of disease created by the overuse of antibiotics given to animals, and the uncertain effects of hormone supplementation and genetically modified feed.

Purposeful ignorance: Given the increased cost of food grown outside the flawed industrial systems,

186

some people choose to bury their heads in the sand to save money. Maybe they place their faith in the FDA and the USDA...but these are usually the same people who express skepticism the government could properly accomplish any task, including ensuring the safety of their food supply! I'd heard some truly amazing statements from people who chose the route of purposeful ignorance, "I know how inhumanely Wal-Mart's feeder farms treat their livestock, but I don't care. Just sell me the cheapest meat available." REALLY? You know you get what you pay for, right? And what about your children; are you actually comfortable making this decision for them?

Government's bias toward industrial farming: Big agriculture has a lobby in Washington, the 45 acre poultry farmer does not. The USDA's rules were written to favor the big guys. We operated our farm just fine under the 1,000 bird USDA inspection limit, but if we wanted to raise more birds than that, we had to invest major money in an inherently flawed, interior butchering facility. We had to play by the big boys' rules, and could never compete. To begin with, we couldn't break-even selling chicken at commercial prices; we had more money invested in feed than a commercial chicken's entire price per pound.

We wanted consumers to support family farms instead of big corporations. Our livelihood came from what we produced. We were not in business to pass profits through to some suits in an office tower. We charged the true cost of food; grown with care, humanely, and at a scale that ensured a quality product rather than an antibiotic and hormone ridden

187

product of the CAFO's. The cost of industrial food is artificially low, with feed subsidized by government programs and costs saved via inhumane environments: pigs and cows grown in conditions where they can barely move; poultry grown in stacked cages where they defecate on each other, breathe manure dust all their lives, and cannot even take a step due to overcrowding, all in the name of profit.

Decades ago, Americans sacrificed the quality of their food to industrial efficiency, lulled by the clever marketing of big agribusiness. The cost of food had been held artificially low all those years through misguided government subsidization.

Daniel and I parted that Saturday morning equally passionate about the importance of our callings. I had one argument to bypass all this high-minded talk; specific to chickens but adaptable to any livestock: Would you eat a chicken that was covered in shit and breathed chicken shit dust all its life and lived in darkness, or would you prefer to eat a chicken that lived its life breathing fresh air, living in sunshine, eating green grass, was humanely cared for and butchered, and was sold to you by the person who ensured the chicken lived this way? Do you think such a chicken would taste better? How much more is that chicken worth to you? And how much does supporting a local farmer, versus a faceless, distant corporation, mean to you?

Fifteen

The sun beat on the hot pavement at the Triphammer Farmers Market and Patty, the egg lady, was talking again. Sometimes I liked to sit and take in the scene, or read a book during slow times, but Patty always liked to talk. She had the tent next door to mine. Her plastic bins were filled with knitted mittens, hats, and dish towels, and she had a couple of coolers of eggs priced by size. The knitted stuff was a hard sell in the August heat.

Patty was the salt of the earth, in her 60's, and worried about her and her husband's future. He worked for the Homer highway department and wanted to retire. She didn't know how they would make ends meet. Over the course of the summer I listened to Patty's life stories and her worries. I liked talking to Patty despite my tendency to drift off once in a while. I sympathized with her situation.

Patty was the one who had assailed me with business planning questions the first day I visited the market. Now I understood why: she was trying to figure out how to make a living from her two acre place. Two acres could be a little or a lot of land depending on what you were growing. A lot of hoop houses could be built on two acres. There was a local CSA that provided 1,100 families with produce from just seven acres. On the other hand, two acres was way too small for a cattle or field crop operation. Our farm, at 45 acres, was called Just a Few Acres because it was small for my parents' use of it as a field crop and beef cattle farm, but it fit poultry farming just fine. Patty liked growing chickens and rabbits, and I believed she could make it work on two acres. Convincing her was the hard part.

She had 70 free range laying chickens and a few rabbits. I never considered laying chickens to be a significant income generator. They were better used as an entry product, a door opener to introduce other products to new customers. Laying chickens, when used in combination with other farm ventures, could also perform important services that didn't appear on a balance sheet. We planned on using our layers to remove insect larvae and to spread out cattle manure on our pastures once we began raising beef cattle. They were also great at tearing up the plants and loosening the soil of vegetable gardens at the end of the year, fertilizing them in the process.

Patty was barely making enough money from her egg sales to cover her feed bills and her gasoline to get to market. I wondered why she even bothered to drive 20 miles from Homer to the Ithaca market, burning $8 in gasoline round trip, to sell 30 dozen eggs at a profit of around $1/dozen. Her rabbits, I told her, were where she could make some money, and this depended on one of the first principles of direct marketing: value added services.

My Great Grandmother made money selling canned rabbit. She raised, butchered, cooked, deboned, and canned the meat, and sold it ready to eat all from our farm. The same applied to her butter: she raised the cows, milked them, separated the cream, churned the butter, bulk stored it in lard-sealed crocks, and portioned it for sale. The supply chain was simple; she grew and processed products from start to finish. This was direct marketing; she was connected directly to her consumers with no middlemen to take pieces of the profit pie.

If she sold her rabbits to a butcher or her butter to a grocer, she would have made less profit on her products (assuming she was efficient at processing and sales), because she would have had to sell at wholesale rather than retail prices. In addition, she was providing value added services. She could have sold her milk to customers, and they could have separated the cream and churned their own butter, but instead she invested in a mechanical cream separator and captured the extra profit from the processing steps she brought within her control. The same with her rabbits. Key to her success in these extra steps was her expertise at them; she knew the best ways to make butter and cook rabbit, and the finished products tasted better than most of her customers could have produced themselves.

My Great Grandmother was not unique. In her time, many products moved from farm to table locally. But things changed with the industrialization of agriculture. Industrial broiler production is a good example. Typically, the grower never even owns the chickens she/he grows. The parent corporation engages the grower to provide the service of housing and growing their chickens. They provide the specifications for the growing facility; the farmer spends hundreds of thousands of dollars to construct it, and is paid only to raise the livestock. He captures no value-added services (except possibly a bonus for chicken mortality below his contract percentage). The farmer is at the mercy of the corporation; she/he has no recourse if abandoned by their patron beyond the initial contract period; does not have the resiliency of a wide customer base.

Patty wanted to make the same mistake as the poor poultry grower; she did not seem to understand what gave my Great Grandmother's generation resiliency and independence. I was passionate about our rights as farmers to reclaim this independence from big agribusiness and the inhuman market forces of the modern economy. Every winter she allowed herself to be manipulated by her customers into selling her eggs at wholesale prices, because they knew she was having a hard time selling her eggs without the weekly summer markets. I told her these were no customers to have; if they didn't understand the difference between her free range eggs and those of the big box stores, then she should either find new customers who valued her product, freeze her extra stock, or donate it to the local food pantry. She was cheapening herself and the image of the local foods movement by putting herself in competition with the industrial food system.

And her rabbits! Her plan was to sell them to pet stores and on Craigslist. Several times during the summer she told me she had a buyer from Craigslist who was to pick up rabbits, and they never showed. The same thing had happened to me selling household items on Craigslist; I would never sell farm products there. Again, it was a matter of image; we were not selling a commodity, we were selling a healthier food future. It had no place at auctions and flea markets. Its value was not negotiable. I couldn't get Patty to see the nuance.

I reviewed the business and marketing plan with her as I would execute it. First, rabbit meat was hard to find in our area, so it could command a premium price. $6 per pound was a good starting point. It could be sold as a novelty, and a repeat customer base could be developed if the meat was uniquely delicious and had an environmentally conscious story: pastured rabbit for example. Second, rabbits carry all their fat in their viscera. Their meat is extremely lean and healthy. Tell customers about that, along with the rabbits' light footprint on the environment. Start a trend about an overlooked old-time food. Like chickens, rabbits grow very fast. And, better than chickens, a greater percentage of their diet could come straight from pasture; straight from current solar income and the forage that synthesized it. Finally, since customers were not familiar with how to prepare rabbit, provide an education: let them know how simple it is to slow cook and take the meat from the bones; what a delicious stew it made or how it could be added into other dishes after stewing.

Sell rabbit with all the value that could be added. Unlike chickens, rabbits do a fine job at breeding quickly; there are no expenses in buying young rabbits. Chicks had to be shipped from the hatchery at $1.00+ each. However, unfortunately and unlike chickens, rabbits had to be butchered in a USDA inspected facility. Why this was, I could not guess any more than the many other vagaries of government control that strangled the small farmer's ability to make a living. Anyway, find a butcher to dress the rabbits and package them whole, then sell them directly to consumers.

I do not know why, but Patty never saw the sense in my advice, or maybe she saw the sense but was overwhelmed by starting such an operation. I tucked the business plan away as a possible future venture for our farm. I believed there was a market niche to be filled. I saw similar niches in ducks and geese. Each required consumer education, but after all, wasn't that the pinch point in the entire local foods movement? Getting consumers to understand the wide ranging positive implications of eating local had become critical to the expansion of our customer base.

*   *   *

One cold January morning, I cracked walnuts in the workshop and thought about economic growth. I had come back to this topic many times over the past five years, and never had a good answer. Economic growth was tied to increasing production and consumption, which was tied to greater prosperity, which ultimately led back to the extraction at increasing rates of the Earth's natural resources. That was the problem of growth.

Environmentalists had repeated for decades that infinite growth on a finite planet was impossible. Of course they were right, but it was not a pleasant message for folks to hear, and nobody seemed to have a palatable alternative to the old tried-and-true equations of economic growth and its relationship to increasing prosperity. Some environmentalists thought steady-state economies (zero overall growth) were the answer; I had participated in discussions at some of the conferences I attended regarding how they could work. Steady-state economies implied stagnation and required more government control than I could stomach.

When I was an architect, our firm's accountant stressed the importance of our firm's economic growth. Here's where the issue really hit home. He said the only way we could make room for younger folks to advance up the corporate ladder, and to provide raises for everyone, was to either increase the firm's gross revenue or become more efficient given a flat gross revenue, thereby increasing our net revenue. In my twenty years, I witnessed a combination of

195

both; we grew 750% in gross revenue, and we all ran faster on the treadmill to increase our efficiency; our net revenue. The result was financial growth accompanied by much stress and a dim future of running faster and faster. I wished for an alternative.

While cracking walnuts, it occurred to me if I crossed the concepts of value added services and increased gross revenue with my pride in producing food on the farm, versus consuming resources as an architect, a bit of magic happened. Most simply, it meant America needs to reverse its trend toward consumption back toward production. The execution of this is far from simple.

First, America has long undervalued craft. Craft is pride in the making of things; production. High school shop classes and vocational schools are mostly populated by those who feel they have no other future. Intelligent and creative young people need to discover the satisfaction and creativity of working with their hands, making something! College is not the only route for America's bright and talented. The blue collar world has long been populated by those who see it as a way to make a living, without pride of craft. This is not their fault. Our society has long undervalued craft, instead favoring bigger, cheaper, and shoddier. They are running faster on the treadmill, just as I had in the white collar world, and the sacrifice of quality and pride are the consequences. Meanwhile, other countries are beating America in the quality and low cost of the products they produce; cars from Japan, TV's from South Korea, and almost everything else from China. I am witnessing a revaluing of craft in America's young farmers; this needs to spread to the other hands-on trades.

I know people who will only buy American-made products, and admire their resolve. I want to buy as local as possible, but many of America's products are inferior to those of other countries. This is just a fact. Electronics from Asia beat those from America hands down. The styling of American automobiles, and their construction tolerances, can't hold a candle to Asian and European imports. Buying American props up the inherent flaws that have infiltrated American manufacturing; it perpetuates America's inferior products. I can see it in the styling of automobiles especially; they are target-marketed to those of lower incomes and those who remember America's manufacturing dominance of fifty years ago, those who refuse to acknowledge America's decline in manufacturing quality. The only way we will be forced to improve our own products is in the ruthless free-market, free-choice economy. Once again, this led me to the conclusion that America's best and brightest should be reengaged in the making of things, rather than entering its dominant service and consumption based professions.

The key to America's economic growth is not how much we consume. I am tired of hearing our economic success depends on Black Friday and Christmas season sales. Most of the products purchased are being made overseas! Many of our purchasing dollars are leaving our country! Bring manufacturing back to the US! But don't do it in the traditional way – by increasing import tariffs into the US. Make US products what they once were: the highest quality in the world. Make them worth the money charged for them. Avoid the trap of competing with Chinese government subsidization, low wages, and unfair tariffs, by bringing America's best and brightest back to the manufacturing sector. Take pride in what we make! I am seeing it happen in the local farm movement; I know it can translate to other production endeavors.

On the surface, the restoration of production to consumption is a simple way to grow our economy without asking people to consume more, as we have for decades. A return to America producing and consuming its own products is a giant case of value added services, and a massive increase in the availability of jobs as people return to manufacturing. If we can make what we sell, then we can capture more profit from a start-to-finish production, marketing, and sales system, following my example of my great grandmother and her rabbits.

Further down, it diversifies the American definition of success that jumped the tracks decades ago. Making things, and innovating in the making of things, is what built our country, and a return to valuing that could both bring our country back to the forefront of manufacturing, and give our bright young people an alternative to the white collar, college-bound, one size fits all, version of the American dream.

Sixteen

On August seventh, six months to the day after taking my leave of absence, I drove to Cortland to have lunch with Ed McGraw. Ed was the firm's CEO (chief executive officer). He and I had become good friends during our twenty years in business together, and he was always supportive of my work. Ed and I met many times during my leave of absence. Sometimes he visited the farm for lunch, and sometimes I met him in Syracuse for lunch. Today's meeting was an emergency. I had texted him the evening before, and he'd agreed to meet in Cortland today.

Six months had passed in a hurry. I thought back on them as a series of discrete phases. The first two months I wandered, quietly recovered, and washed myself of negativity. At the two month mark I found a direction: farming. The next three months were an exciting period of the farm's growth, talking about its possibilities with Hilarie, becoming a part of the community, and starting to sell our products. The last month had been a gut-grinding period of indecision.

My leave had changed my life. It refocused my priorities and stripped away some of the "noise" of modernity that had confused me at work. I stood on solid ground now, confident in my calling to farm and to be home with my family, but I had taken several leaps to get to that ground, and would need to take some more leaps in the future, the first one coming at today's lunch. To change my life, I had to take some risks. I had to trust that if I was doing what I was meant to do, the universe would somehow make it possible for me to do so. I had to have faith that when I took a leap things would arrange themselves so I landed on solid ground.

When I left architectural work in February I took my first leap. I told myself, "This is not working, and I need time to figure out what to do." The leap had nothing to do with my job security; I was pretty sure my partners would welcome me back at the end of a six month absence. The leap I took was in not knowing how I would take care of my family's financial needs. The firm stepped up to help me there, continuing our health insurance and some of the other perks of being a principal. Other insurance stepped in to meet the rest of our needs.

The next leap I took was starting the farm. I didn't just stick my toe in the water when I made this decision; I jumped right into it. I knew it was the right thing to do; it was a reawakening of something that had long slept within me, since childhood. It was the most honest and humble way to practice and further develop the ideas I had developed in architecture. I moved from the consumption side of the scale to the production side. I had felt guilty about architecture's basic foundations in natural resource consumption. How good it felt to produce healthy, responsible food and to heal our land and build community while doing so! Hilarie and the kids were right there with me on this leap. It felt right to all of us.

Still, I didn't know what to do about the coexistence of my previous life in architecture with my new life in farming. I pushed it to the back of my mind for most of my leave. I thought the answer would present itself when the right time came. But during the month of July, the last of the six months, I chewed on the issue day after day. It turns out what I was really doing was agonizing over the leap my inner self already knew I needed to take. This would be the biggest leap of all. A few weeks before Ed's and my meeting in Cortland, I had tried to take a leap without taking a leap.

Two weeks earlier, on July twenty-third I had met with Ed to open the discussion of the terms of my return. We had lunch together at a restaurant in Syracuse. We had an exciting conversation. I presented that I wanted to farm part-time, and work at the firm part-time. The balance of the two would be seasonally dependent: summers would be almost full-time farming, winters almost full-time at the firm. I would sell my ownership in the firm, and work as a consultant, focusing on the work in architecture I most enjoyed: discovering the deeper philosophical opportunities each project held, helping project teams to translate that philosophy into built form, and working with a small group of employees to further develop our philosophy.

Ed and I were both excited by the potential of this arrangement, and he began suggesting other things I could do at the firm: finish the book my team and I had started writing, resume the seminars I provided to the firm, begin traveling and lecturing again, start attending key client meetings to help move their decision-making toward the design philosophy we wished to express. It seemed like everything was coming together for me; a life combining what I loved about both farming and architecture, and I could control their balance. After two hours of conversation, Ed and I parted, both of us happy with the lunch's outcome. I would return to work in September, after Labor Day.

I returned home and gave Hilarie the good news. She asked if I was sure I was comfortable with things (Hil and I had talked about the proposed arrangement before I met with Ed; to make sure we were in agreement). I replied I was thrilled! We could have our life on the farm with no worries about our finances. How could it have worked out any better? She was happy for me, but not as happy as I expected. Something was going on here...

After the July twenty-third meeting I returned to the rhythm of chores, projects, and markets. I received messages from Deborah Rhea and a few other friends at the firm who were glad to hear of my return. But I started experiencing episodes of great anxiety so intense they were accompanied by pain in the middle of my chest. What was causing this? They grew progressively worse. I knew how to deal with these feelings. I had experienced them before and knew the key was to identify the source of the anxiety. No matter how random and disconnected the episodes were, there was a cause I needed to identify. Simply identifying the cause would lessen them, and proactively dealing with the cause would eventually eliminate them.

I had a new competitor at the Homer market, the first vendor I had encountered who also sold pastured chicken. He had been pushy and rude to me during the last few markets, and at first I thought this was the source of the anxiety. But it was not. (By the way, we became friends soon after that. First impressions aren't everything.)

I concentrated on my feelings regarding returning to work, and found the source of the anxiety. Deep down, I had no interest in returning to architecture. In fact, I was inwardly afraid of being forced to do so. How had I ignored this feeling? All the memories of the unhappy days came flooding back. I remembered how I responded throughout my leave when I was asked what I missed about my old job: Nothing, except a few friends. I had compromised who I was meant to be for the sake of financial security; my subconscious was practically screaming it at me.

There was no way around it; I had to take the biggest leap of all. My inner self would allow nothing else.

I pulled into a parking spot on Main Street in

Cortland on August seventh with complete resolve. Ed was already at the restaurant. He knew why we were meeting before I said anything. I was not coming back. I would sell my ownership, and asked that the firm continue our health insurance through the end of the year, pay off my car, and take care of the final year of my corporate tax preparation. Ed graciously took the news. As my friend, he wanted me to be happy more than anything to do with the business. He saw how I had changed in the last six months, and knew I had found the right path. I had had a one in a million job, had owned a firm with some of the most caring, gracious people I had ever met. They let me go with their full support. I am forever thankful to them for that.

My leaving the firm did not end my relationships with these friends. Many friendships at work depend on the common experiences of life at work. They give us things to talk about and pull us together as we experience hard times. Without that commonality, the relationships start to fade. I found this to be the case with some of my old friendships. But others, happily, continued strong. I still saw Deborah and Bob Rhea every week, had occasional lunches with some of my old partners, sent our farm's products up to Syracuse for sale at the firm, and received visitors from the firm who wanted to see the farm. The firm partnership even asked us to grow holiday turkeys for all 50 employees of the firm next year.

The final leap was the one I tried to hedge my bets against – having my cake and eating it too – by combining the financial security of my old life with the meaningfulness of my new life. It just couldn't be done. My subconscious knew it, and I should have too. My prior work told me that. Another facet of the philosophy I developed at work, possibly the largest, most overarching one, was *synthesis*. It was certainly at play in my final business discussions with Ed.

Synthesis was the guidepost signaling our arrival at a new, different future. In architecture, it was the concept I had the most difficulty explaining to others. Synthesis was the combination of many formerly discrete factors into a singular, inseparable whole. It was the merging of a new architectural design value set with environmental considerations.

Synthesis was the opposite of the current state of green building design, where new technology was being tacked onto old design systems (the most obvious example being the addition of solar panels on roofs), or building elements were being swapped out for more environmentally friendly ones: naturally sourced linoleum for vinyl composition floor tile, low VOC (volatile organic compound) paints for oil-based paints, bamboo for hardwoods, etc. I (and others) called these buildings "Frankensteins:" assemblages of odd pieces never designed to be bolted together.

The last time synthesis had occurred in architecture was in the 1920's, when new materials and building systems such as float glass, steel, and curtain wall technology were embraced by a small group of brilliant architects who synthesized this new technology into a completely new design value set: modernism. The time was ripe for this to occur again, moving past modernism's integration with industrialism to a new architecture based on our marriage to nature.

Synthesis was a singular whole, where no component could be removed without compromising the character of the whole. Every component was complementary to the whole. It was psychological harmony. I used the following example in lectures: imagine mixing separate colors of paint or play-doh. At first you can see the separate colors swirling together. This is synthesis in degree: if you had a mind to, you could still separate the component parts. The solar panels could be removed from the building. If you kneaded the play-doh or stirred the paint long enough, eventually you wound up with a single color. Synthesis in this degree was complete and inseparable; the original components could no longer be distinguished or removed.

The achievement of synthesis, which was a singular quality, also required a process which focused on singular qualities, rather than components. I called this process visioning. The secret to achieving synthesis in a building project was to move people away - at least in the early phases – from parts. They needed to be moved to talk about the qualities of the whole: what were the project's aspirations, how did it work with the energies of its place and community, how did it marry itself with the natural world? Vision inherently spoke of synthesis. Both were singular; both held people away from the minutia of everyday concerns – which were important – but needed to be held off until the singular character of the project was determined.

My new life farming was the ultimate synthesis; that which I had searched for in architecture for years. It was the synthesis of self and environment, home and vocation, livelihood and family. No wonder my inner self's defense mechanisms rang at the thought of balancing architecture with farming! Balance was the opposite of synthesis. I wanted a life of singular purpose, uniting family, place, and vocation. And I had found it. A return to architecture was impossible; it would have meant having to balance two worlds.

On August seventh I took my largest leap. There's a funny thing about such leaps; the universe seems to provide for the leaper, if the leaper leaps in the correct direction. Things lined up in our direction in the months succeeding my decision to leave the firm. Our two largest fixed costs, health insurance and property taxes, were greatly reduced through a series of government programs favoring small farmers with low incomes.

Most importantly to me, Hilarie and the kids validated our direction. Cora wrote a letter expressing her love for the farm. Gracie and Henry were eager to start helping with the chores, and followed me around during the day. Hilarie seemed renewed by the prospect of our family living together on the farm, without my absence for twelve hours each day commuting to work in Syracuse.

When I left architecture in February, Hilarie and I were a little worried about how it would affect our relationship. I had always been driven by a clear direction, always knew the next step, always had a plan for the next chunk of free time. What would happen when I lost that direction? Hilarie thought we may wind up bickering during the days we spent at home together. This never happened. Even immediately after I left work, I kept myself busy, mostly out in the workshop, and she was able to continue her daily routine. There was not a single day I spent lying around watching TV during the whole six months.

Hilarie noticed changes in the way I structured my time. Previously, I needed a plan and schedule for everything, and grew anxious if we deviated from the schedule. I loosened up as I let time's flow take me. I could leave a morning project in the middle to go visit a friend. If it was a nasty weather day I could spend the afternoon napping or out at the movies. It's not that my work did not get finished; it was that the work flowed away from fixed schedules. I may have napped on Tuesday afternoon and worked late on Sunday evening. I was able to sit with the kids on a Thursday afternoon and be out to work at 5:30am the next day. Time flowed around and through a life spent in synthesis.

After I made my decision in August not to return to architecture, Hilarie was relieved. For the first time, she told me she had always felt, ever since February, that I should never go back, that the work had damaged me too much. She knew the decision had to come from within me and therefore did not reveal her feelings. My wife is a wise person.

Although Hilarie had no experience with farming, she was confident we had made the right decision, and she shared the view that the proper doors would open for us when needed. In the next few years one or both of us may need to work part-time to make ends meet. Already our lifestyle had changed to conserve money, so we had the freedom to find lower-paying, temporary work during the farm's quieter winter season.

Hilarie was the one who was wisely pulling me to expand our farm quickly. We had expanded our customer base from zero all the way up to all that we could produce in our first year. We were looking at doubling the farm's output in the second year; seizing the opportunity our momentum created. I believed we were on the leading edge of a huge increase in demand for pastured poultry, that it would soon follow the explosion seen in pastured beef production fifteen years ago. Who else was doing what we did in our county? As far as we knew, only a few others, and already we were larger than any of them, and the only to offer a continuous supply. Doors were opening...we just needed to walk through them.

By the end of August, all the paperwork was completed and I was officially no longer associated with the firm. Ed and I resolved to see each other every month or so, just to talk as friends. My six month leave of absence was over, and now time truly stretched before me as a river flowing over the horizon.

Seventeen

One

Sunday morning I was watering trees. Carrying two watering cans, I walked through the tall grass to the tree circle that overlooks the back part of the farm. I looked down to keep my step and continued looking down to water the mulch around the trees. I looked up.

Thousands of small butterflies were hovering over the field, inches above the top of the grass and goldenrod.

These things do not just happen.

It was beautiful. I saw life as a butterfly: careening, jarring, vertiginous. And I thought of Monarch butterflies wavering all the way to Mexico.

Even as each butterfly fluttered, thousands of them made a graceful shimmering veil over the field.

Two

Once a month I mow an adjacent field. The swallows come to eat the bugs that jump from the freshly mowed grass. They fly

211

*around me on the old tractor, gliding and darting, changing
direction on a dime with pointed wings, catching grasshoppers
mid-jump.*

*Their motion is like the script in my great grandmother's
journals: a grace fluid and sweeping.*

<u>Three</u>
*I had a neighbor who was a glider pilot in World War Two.
He flew a two-seater from his grass runway and did barrel rolls
and loop-de-loops. He roared over the farm and we wondered
how much he had drunk that day, and what the chances were of
him hitting the house. We listened to his motor strain arching
upward. He rolled and held at the apex for a moment before
beginning a slow curving glide.*

*Life is motion and change. Its ballet is not on pointed toes.
Fluttering, arching, stuttering; grace in motion lies in its
truthfulness.*

*The grace we each find in motion is its gift to us. Its
expression to others is our gift to the world.*

-"Taking Flight" July 2012

*   *   *

It was late August, and after I finished the morning
chores, I climbed on the Farmall Super C tractor and
headed out to mow the pasture. The tractor had a
four foot brush-hog mower on the back. The mowing
would take almost all day.

I had to mow the pasture every month or so

between April and October. The chickens and turkeys preferred the grasses 3-5" long. When they grew higher than that, they got tougher and the birds would trample them flat instead of grazing them. The exception was alfalfa, their favorite grass. They would pick that clean at any height.

My needing to mow the pasture was an example of an incomplete system. In this case, we were missing a larger grazer such as cattle or sheep, to keep the pasture down. We planned on adding cattle to the system next year. Then, we could alternate meat birds, layers, and cattle in continually changing pasture arrangements, ensuring each type of livestock received the kind of pasture it preferred. This sort of arrangement was what I had in mind when I spoke about pasture systems and livestock systems working together to increase the health of each year after year. Instead of spending money and burning gasoline to mow the pasture, the pasture would be used to convert sunlight into calories consumed by livestock, their grazing would increase the health and density of the pasture grasses, and their manure would gradually increase the fertility of the soil. It is a practical, low cost way to heal the land.

For this and other reasons, mowing is not my favorite job. It was nice enough in the morning, when the temperatures were cool and the grass was wet. I enjoyed watching the swallows dart around the tractor, the sound of the tractor's motor working hard, and being out in the pasture. Later on in the day the job was not so enjoyable. It got hot, the grass dried out and the mower started throwing dust and pollen around, and I became tired of sitting in the tractor's thinly padded seat. It was then I usually started remembering my long and uncomfortable history with mowing fields and making hay.

As soon as I could lift a hay bale, I was conscripted to help Dad and Grandpa during haying season. I must have been six or seven years old; too young to drive the tractor and baler, which was a tricky job. Instead, I was on the hayrack (wagon), stacking the rectangular bales Dad picked up from the field and heaved up to me. Usually there was also an uncle or cousin on the hayrack to help me, especially when I was younger.

Making hay started with cutting the field. Grandpa did this with a sickle bar mower trailing his old Farmall H tractor. The cut grass was left in the field to dry for a few days, depending on the weather. Grandpa joked that every batch of hay needed a good washing by the rain before it was baled, but really its nutrients were best preserved by getting it into the barn before it got rained on.

The hay was usually raked the next day. The rake gathered the hay into windrows and fluffed it for further drying. The windrows trailed down the field like snakes. I was allowed to do the hay raking at a very young age, younger than ten, using the farm's smaller tractor, an Allis Chalmers B. Then came the worst part for me; baling.

Before Grandpa died, we used a New Holland baler hooked to the Farmall H. The baler was powered by the tractor's PTO (power take off), a rotating shaft that came out of the rear of the tractor.

The old Farmall did not have a live PTO. This was always a source of difficulty, and required the tractor operator's complete attention to the status of the baler. A tractor with a live PTO meant the PTO kept turning while the clutch was depressed and the tractor was stopped. When the clutch on the Farmall was depressed, the PTO stopped. The difficulty occurred when the windrow became too large for the baler to keep up, and the tractor operator misjudged the baler's capacity. Sometimes when this happened the baler would become clogged and we had to shut everything down to open its access doors and clean it out. Usually this situation was avoided by having a person holding a pitchfork walk alongside the windrow in front of the baler. The tractor could be popped out of gear without depressing the clutch before it hit the large part of the windrow, then the hay could be forked into the baler at a slower rate. Once this was complete, the tractor was put back in gear and the operation moved ahead.

Dad spent a lot of time walking along the baler watching its knotters while Grandpa drove the tractor. A continuous rectangle of packed hay emerged from the back of the baler. The knotters were complex mechanical devices that kept track of how long each bale should be, and at the end of each bale pulled the baling twine up through the stream of packed hay and tied its knot. There were two of them; making two loops of twine holding each bale together. The knotters were fussy. When they came out of adjustment or got clogged with chaff they wouldn't tie the knot correctly or we'd wind up with

215

really long or short bales. Then the baler was stopped, the knotters repaired, and the goofed-up bales were fed back through the baler.

I have to admit my cousin and I were sometimes the source of the knotters' trouble. By watching Dad we figured out how to keep the mechanism from tripping at the end of a bale, thus creating long snaking bales that fell off the back of the baler. I really did not like haying season.

The baler dropped its hay bales on the ground behind it. If we had enough help, the bales were loaded onto the hayrack and unloaded into the old barn's haymow on the same day, using the smaller Allis Chalmers tractor to pull the wagon. Usually though, the bales were picked up the next day.

I disliked haying season not because of the hard work, but because it made me sick with hay fever. My skin itched when I touched the hay, I felt feverish chills, and my sinuses clogged up. Sometimes when I woke up the next morning my eyes were glued shut with dried drainage; Mom had to clean them with a wet washcloth before I could open them. I especially got sick when we stacked hay in the barn. The air was thick with dust. I itched, sneezed, and shivered until the job was done. I took medicine for the allergies (I remember four separate types taken every day), but it didn't help very much.

When I was older, I went to my Uncle Jim's farm to help him with hay. He had a kicker baler and a hayrack with tall wooden frames on its sides and back. The kicker baler had a spinning set of rubber wheels at the end of its chute, which threw the hay bales up and into the wagon. Uncle Jim controlled the aim of the kicker with a crank on a shaft that went up to his seat on the tractor. The kicker made loading the wagon much easier. I wouldn't really catch the bales (in other words, not stand in front of a 70 pound projectile). Rather, I would move slightly to the side of the bale's trajectory and guide it to land in the correct place with a push. There could be no daydreaming here; if I spent too much time messing with a bale I was in danger of getting knocked over by the next – which sometimes happened.

Dad bought a 1951 Farmall MD tractor and a baler with an air-cooled two cylinder Wisconsin motor after Grandpa died. Both were unique machines. The MD started on gasoline. After it warmed up, two levers had to be pulled at the same time to switch it over to diesel fuel: The first lever engaged the diesel injector pump and closed a valve in each cylinder's combustion chamber that housed a spark plug, also increasing the tractor's compression ratio so it could ignite diesel fuel. The second lever throttled the motor all the way open. I think that tractor started my love affair with antique Farmalls; the sound it made when those two levers were pulled and it roared to life made my spine tingle.

MD's were notoriously hard to start when the weather was cold. The idea behind their starting on gasoline was to warm up the engine so it could burn diesel fuel, but they were hard to start even on gasoline when it was cold.

The baler's Wisconsin motor was cantankerous as well, except in the opposite way. The motor sat on top of the front of the baler, and had a flywheel on its front. It was started by pulling on the flywheel by hand, like starting an old airplane by pulling on its propeller. The motor almost always started easily, but shutting it off when it was hot was a big mistake; it would not start again until it cooled down.

During the summer, either when I got home from high school or in the early afternoon during summer vacation, I baled hay while Dad was at work. We baled from our land, and also from a neighbor's land a few miles away. Since the baler had its own motor, it eliminated the problems we used to have with Grandpa's PTO driven baler. If I got into a thick section of windrow, I could slip the clutch on the tractor or put it into a lower gear without stopping the baler's power source. I enjoyed baling hay with this equipment.

When Dad got home we loaded hay onto his old pickup truck and stacked it in the pole barn. This was much less dusty than the enclosed haymow in the old barn. I think my allergies lessened as I got older too, although they still bother me. I actually missed these days making hay after I went to college and Dad stopped farming. The MD still sits in the last bay of the pole barn, waiting for me to restore it someday.

My affection for old tractors never went away. The 1953 International Harvester Farmall Super C I was using to mow the pasture was one of about ten old Farmalls I collected during the years before we started farming. At first I enjoyed fully restoring them: tearing them completely apart, cleaning, repairing or replacing parts, rebuilding motors and transmissions,

218

and painting them. Just like the clocks I repaired, the worse shape the tractor started out in, the more I enjoyed the work. They looked new when I was finished. Later, I grew to appreciate their original appearance; rusty, dented, and greasy, because it was richer; it showed the tractor's years of hard work. Then I focused only on repairing their mechanical issues. The Super C was in this latter group.

The oldest tractor I owned was a 1924 McCormick Deering 10-20 with steel wheels. It drove like a tank. The three tractors I used most often were built in 1940, 1949, and 1953. I cannot imagine anything, including a tractor, being built today that would still be in use 75 years later, as these tractors were. The reason was that, in general, as the things we make have grown more natural resource efficient, they have become less resilient. Old tractors are incredibly resilient, but extremely resource inefficient. They were over-engineered, using a lot more metal than was required, and did not use fuel as efficiently as today's tractors do.

When I was an architect, resiliency was a perennial topic in sustainable design, and I often used the example of old tractors to illustrate some of the tensions inherent in the efficiency vs. resiliency conversation. Here are definitions of the two terms:

Resilient: Withstanding stress and catastrophe. *This was a common definition, and it reminded me of a boat that stayed afloat in a storm. I would rather it said something about adapting and thriving through change, which is what we really needed to do.*

Efficient: Achieving maximum production with minimum waste.

To be resilient has tremendous implications on sustainable design. The buildings and communities we design need to withstand, adapt, and (hopefully) thrive through all sorts of change: climate change, natural resource availability change, and social change to name a few.

There is a sense of safety in resiliency; that we can weather any storm. This is part of why doomsday prepping has entered the popular consciousness and resiliency is in the Boy Scouts' motto; it is empowering.

Efficiency has the opposite effect; as efficiency increases, the danger of failure under unforeseen conditions increases. Our pattern has been to build less and less resiliency, and more and more efficiency into things as time has progressed; it has allowed us to make more things using the same amount of resources, and to operate those things using less energy. Compare an old tractor to a Prius automobile; one is simple, resilient, and inefficient, the other is complicated, efficient, and non-resilient. I can fix a tractor under a shady tree with a few tools. The Prius has to go back to the dealer to be hooked into a diagnostic computer by a mechanic with years of training.

Then I added tightness of fit to the conversation. When we make things most efficiently, they fit their end use tightly. When we design an efficient building, part of its efficiency is the result of how tightly it fits its occupants' needs. We ask exactly what hours and days the building will be used, and the specifications of the computers and other equipment that will be plugged in. We also fine-tune the building to its climate, using historical climate data. Tightness of fit increases efficiency, but works against resiliency. What would happen if the average yearly temperature went up three degrees, or if the occupancy hours were changed? The building would not operate within the narrow parameters it was designed to, and the result could be less efficient performance.

Old-timers say, "They don't make things like they used to." They are right; old things (not only tractors) usually last longer than new things because old things were built to looser tolerances, which means they can accommodate more wear, with operational inefficiency (consumption of fuel and oil) as a consequence. And they were built with more redundancy and less efficient use of initial natural resources (iron and steel) in their manufacture. Metallurgy was not as sophisticated as it is today, so parts were designed more robustly to make up for possible defects in steel and cast iron. Farmers did things with tractors that the designers could not anticipate, so tractors were designed to take unintended stresses. The quality of available fuel and oil varied widely so carburetors were designed to run on a broad range, cylinder compression ratios were low, oil capacities were large and moving part tolerances loose. Maintenance was often by the farmer, whose primary business was farming, not mechanical work, so systems were kept simple. All together this resulted in a machine that was not an efficient use of resources by any modern analysis, but was robustly designed and therefore resilient enough to be functioning 70 years or more after it was manufactured.

The old timers were right, but unfortunately the good old days of robust engineering are largely in the past for a couple of good reasons:

- It flies in the face of resource efficiency and the almighty "lowest first cost" that drives consumer markets
- Change began to happen too fast. Maybe I could take a guess at what a tractor might look like in 50 years, but a computer? A car? A phone? Not a clue.

These discussions set up a necessary tension between resiliency and efficiency. In architecture, we know we have to design buildings that are both efficient and resilient, so they consume the minimum amount of natural resources and can function under the conditions of an uncertain future. Some people have trouble with this tension; they want to focus on one or the other, efficiency or resiliency. But some tensions are just fine to hold without resolution, and the continuing exploration of their relationship can be a generous source of creativity.

Sitting on the Super C mowing the pasture, I thought about my architectural efficiency-resiliency discussions in light of our farming activities. My decision-making had crossed back and forth between various combinations of the two. Our home favored natural resource efficiency with its solar power and reused materials, and resiliency with its wood stove heating. Our adaptable farm structures, our old tractors, and our attitude toward banking nutrients in the soil favored resiliency also. With each choice, I had weighed the merits of possible paths and chose the one most suited to us and best for the land. I didn't feel the tension of resiliency and efficiency pulling at each other as I had felt in architecture.

I noticed our attitude towards the land always landed on the side of increasing its resiliency via banking nutrients and increasing soil health. This contrasted with industrial farming's focus on efficiency. Efficiency bulldozed the hedgerows that provided rich habitat for birds and other beneficial species. Efficiency used fossil fuel based fertilizers and genetically engineered crops. Efficiency concentrated dairy herds in huge barns and spread their hormone-laden liquid manure over thousands of acres. Efficiency created giant farms and severed the direct connection between farmer and consumer. Hilarie and I were investing in our family's and our land's future by focusing on resiliency.

Eighteen

"The elderberries are ripe!" I told Hilarie when I came in from morning chores to eat breakfast one mid-August day. I passed the bushes every day on my way back to the pasture, and had been watching the berries' progress for the last few weeks. "Well, some of them are, anyway." Thus began wine and cider making season.

After breakfast, I headed into the garden with a stainless steel bowl for berry picking. We had ten elderberry bushes, planted three years earlier along the back garden fence. They had grown fast, sending out runners to sprout new bushes every spring. They grew so fast the overpopulated and ravenous deer could not even keep up with them. Thus they were designated a deer resistant species even as the deer munched on their branches in the wintertime. Next spring, I planned on separating some of the runners to transplant into the beginnings of a new hedgerow running down to the woods at the back of our property. Maybe they could even be woven into living fences like those used in Europe.

The elderberries were the latest addition to August's garden bounty. Hilarie was picking tomatoes every day. She canned some into salsa and general purpose marinara sauce, and we blanched, chopped, and vacuum packed some for the red clam and puttanesca sauces I made during the fall and winter. Collards, swiss chard, arugula, Simpson, romaine, and Waldmann's lettuces, and radishes had been coming continuously out of the chicken coop garden since May, which caught enough shade to keep the cool weather early and late season crops going all summer. These came straight to our table every evening as salads and sautéed greens.

What little sweet corn we had planted had been exceptional this year, with each stalk delivering two or three ears of corn. The kids loved sweet corn more than anything else from the garden. Cora, our pickiest eater, could eat a half dozen ears at one sitting. We stir fried red and green bell peppers with summer squash, chicken breast and our own fresh herbs; we picked basil and parsley from the coop garden for fresh pesto once a week. Soon we would be digging pumpkins, and acorn, butternut, and Boston Marrow squash out of the weedy squash patches and drying them on wire racks; cooking, mashing and freezing the butternut; and roasting the other squash as it cured and sweetened until the first hard freezes in November.

Elderberries favor moist soil, naturally sprouting

along swamp edges and creek banks. In the spring, I had run a soaker hose along the row of bushes, and laid down cardboard and wood mulch to keep their roots moist. We hadn't had any long droughts this summer. I was looking at a bumper crop of berries, and those berries would make our finest variety of homemade wine.

Elderberries are somewhat tricky to harvest. Their berries do not all ripen at the same time. Even a given panicle (cluster) of berries usually did not ripen all at the same time. Folks disagreed on when a berry was ripe. Some favored color (purple), others looseness on the stem, still others looked for the birds to take a few as a sign of proper picking time. I trusted my taste buds; picked a berry, tasted a little sweetness and the correct softness, and away I went. This was like tuning a guitar; eating a few berries at the beginning of each day's picking tuned my eyes to the correct ones to pick.

To pick the berries, sections of panicles or whole panicles of berries were cut from the plant with a pair of shears, and the panicles fell into a bowl held below. Once I had picked all the ripe berries of the day, I brought the bowl into the house and Hilarie and I (and sometimes Grace) separated the berries from the stems by rolling our fingers around clusters of berries, staining our fingers purple for the morning. There were sometimes hundreds of berries on a panicle. The berries dropped off the stems into another bowl, then we combined our bowls and the day's take of berries was added to the collection of gallon Ziploc bags full of berries in the freezer.

We harvested berries as they became ripe every morning throughout the remainder of August and into September. When the bushes were stripped clean, we had 14 pounds of berries in the freezer. It may not sound like much, but it would make eight gallons of wine, or forty bottles, made in two runs of four gallons each.

Hilarie and I made wine from anything but grapes, focusing on lesser known old-time varieties. In the spring, we made dandelion wine. In the fall, we made sour cherry, pumpkin, and elderberry wine, and hard cider. During the winter, we fermented mead, made from honey. At any given time throughout the year, we had between ten and forty gallons of wine or cider fermenting in the basement wine cellar, and about 300 bottles (and growing) of wine aging.

Hilarie favored our pumpkin wine; I liked our mead the best. I have a feeling those with seasoned noses would have preferred our elderberry. After it aged, it had a beautiful deep purplish-red color and complex flavor. We finished it to the dry end of the scale, which could remove the subtlety from cider or mead, but the elderberries' body handled nicely.

In November, after things had slowed down on the farm, I started making wine. The chest freezers held bags of frozen, grated pumpkin and elderberries. I bottled the eight gallons of dandelion which had been bulk aging in the five gallon glass carboys since May, then I set to work starting the batches of new wine, starting with the pumpkin.

Making wine, no matter the variety, followed the same basic process for the home winemaker. First, the ingredients were mixed in a large plastic bucket and yeast was added ("pitched") to start primary fermentation. In the case of pumpkin, I placed the grated pumpkin, along with raisins, in a polyester fermentation bag sealed with a zip tie into the fermentation bucket, and added five gallons of boiling water, cinnamon sticks, peeled ginger root, and nutmeg seeds. After the mixture cooled I added sugar to bring it up to the proper specific gravity, using a hydrometer to measure. The beginning specific gravity would determine the wine's final alcohol content, usually between 11 and 14%. Then I pitched the yeast, covered the bucket with a cotton cloth, and let the yeast do its thing...rapidly multiplying over the next few days, gobbling up the sugar, and excreting alcohol and carbon dioxide.

During primary fermentation the mixture would foam and fizz. The buckets were in the pantry and we could hear their fizz from the kitchen. Once a day I stirred the bag of pumpkin and raisins around and the bucket filled with foam from escaping carbon dioxide. After three or four days the mixture would reach its "2/3 sugar break," the point at which the hydrometer showed the yeast had consumed 2/3 of the mixture's sugar. Now it was time to start secondary fermentation.

Whereas primary fermentation in the plastic bucket had allowed oxygen from the air into the "must" (the wine mixture), secondary fermentation would remove oxygen from the process; turning the yeast from aerobic to anaerobic fermentation. This would prevent oxidation of the wine. I siphoned the must

229

from the plastic bucket into a carboy; a five gallon glass container with a narrow neck. All equipment was carefully sanitized. The carboy was sealed with a rubber stopper with a hole in the middle, into which was inserted an airlock; a u-shaped disinfectant-filled trap that allowed CO_2 to escape the carboy, but no new air to enter. The must in the carboy was stored in the basement wine room, bubbling away for months and occasionally "racked" (siphoned) into a new glass carboy, removing the must from the lees (sediment made up of dead yeast and other solids that had dropped out of the liquid) that had accumulated at the bottom of the carboy.

Eventually the yeast would finish its work and the airlock would stop bubbling. If all went right, the dead yeast would settle to the bottom of the carboy and the wine would clear. At this time the wine was completely dry, assuming the yeast had not reached its upper alcohol limit and it had eaten all the sugar. The clear wine was racked off the lees a final time, stabilized with campden and sorbate to keep the yeast from reactivating, backsweetened to taste with sugar or honey, and bottled. Then it aged for varying periods; pumpkin a year (if we could wait that long), mead a year or two, and elderberry six months.

With all wines except mead, two "runs" were made during primary fermentation. That is, once the must was siphoned off into the carboy, a fresh batch of water and sugar would be added back into the primary bucket containing the bag with the pumpkin, elderberries, or whatever type of wine was being made, and a second fermentation made from the mix.

During secondary fermentation, the two runs would be blended into a single batch.

This year's bumper crop of apples threw a wrench into my wine making routine. I usually fermented three or four gallons of apple cider in one gallon carboys, but this year cider was coming free for the taking, if you knew the right people.

Over the summer, Keith and I had become friends with John and Karen McGillen, who lived in Trumansburg, about a half hour's drive away on the other side of Ithaca. They had a booth at the Triphammer Market, and sold lamb, fruits, and vegetables. The first time I met them, I asked John what all he grew on his farm. He replied, "We're homesteaders." That summed it up well. About four years ago, they had taken early retirement from their jobs in Maryland (John worked for the state's wastewater regulation agency, and Karen was a substitute teacher), bought a 52 acre farm, and began living with less and producing much of their own food.

As homesteaders, John and Karen had a little bit of everything on their farm, including some clever inventions using found materials. They had a nice old farmhouse and timber framed barns. They had large vegetable gardens, old orchards, sheep, cattle, chickens, and ducks. They had a chicken plucker made from two old bench grinders mounted to a table with a piece of PVC pipe between, into which slots had been cut and pieces of rubber tie-downs a few inches long (minus the metal hooks at their ends) inserted. The grinders served as the plucker's bearings. An electric motor with a belt drove one of the grinders. The pipe spun and the rubber straps whirled. The chicken was held near the plucker and rotated as the whirling straps took its feathers off.

They had (as John called it) a "hillbilly hot tub," a stock watering tank with piping that looped down a nearby metal stovepipe connected to a concrete block firebox. The water in the loop was driven by a pond pump. They sat in the open-topped stock tank filled with water heated by the wood fire. The firebox doubled as the heat source for their evaporator during maple syrup season. A rectangular stainless steel pan was put on top of the concrete blocks and a beer keg cut in half with a valve near its bottom sat above one end, dripping fresh sap into the pan to be boiled.

Their pastures were beautiful, the healthiest I had ever seen. Their 30 sheep and five Dexter cattle were kept together in a small paddock enclosed by electric net fencing. The paddock was moved every morning. Once a paddock was grazed, it was left to rest for at least 35 days. The livestock ate only pasture, with no grain supplement. In the winter they ate only hay, taken off the same land. The results were amazing; the pasture looked like none of the "traditional" pastures seen on most farms. Instead of close-cropped grass (and usually some mud, burdock, and thistle), the pasture was filled with a bright green, dense polyculture of forage species. The livestock was healthy and clean. The fast paddock rotation reduced the need for parasite control medications. Parasites were a common problem in sheep. By moving the sheep from the manure they had deposited on the pasture the previous day, parasite eggs in the manure were less likely to infect other sheep.

The Dexter cattle were used to guard the sheep from predators, coyotes mainly. I fell in love with the Dexters the first time I saw them at John's. They are a small, dual purpose breed (milk and meat) originally from Ireland. They were peaceful and friendly; I could walk right up to them and pet them without them becoming the least bit skittish. John wanted to sell two bred cows and I hoped to have them on our pasture next spring, completing our grazing system.

John and Karen also had a large cider press that was over 100 years old, on "permanent loan" from a neighbor. The press could hold 150 pounds of apples at one time which, when pressed, yielded about ten gallons of cider.

And they had a lot of apples to press! Some of their trees were so large I couldn't put my arms around their trunks, and they were all loaded with apples this season. Fridays at market through October and into November, John and Karen gave us an update on how much cider they had made. 20 gallons, 50 gallons...on up past 100 gallons by mid November, and still going. They were realizing they would not be able to get it all in by winter. John invited Keith and I over to make cider for ourselves. "Free," John said, "this is what is right to do when you have overabundance."

On a cool sunny morning in mid November Keith and I pulled into John and Karen's driveway. Their half dozen ducks wandered the yard in a group, waddling and quacking. John and Karen were already at work, collecting fallen apples in a wheelbarrow from a tree in the side yard. The old press was set up on one side of the driveway, with John's homemade apple grinder beside it. There was a table for sorting apples, and crates full of apples here and there.

First I had to see their new chicks. The last time we had visited one of their hens was brooding on about 20 eggs in the field. Three of the eggs had hatched, and now the chicks were three weeks old. Chicks the old fashioned way instead of from the hatchery! The hen had great mothering instincts, although she had never been mothered herself. Usually chicks were hatched from an incubator and raised in heated brooders, with no mother hens around, as ours were. She stayed with her chicks to protect them from the other chickens, and to let them crawl under her for warmth when needed. They moved in and out of the doorway of the chicken coop. Karen said that a few days ago the chicks had ventured outside for the first time.

John had offered to give us 20 gallons of cider, which we would press that morning in two batches. We collected fallen apples from two trees near the press using the wheelbarrow. Next we washed the apples in a large tub of water and sorted them: good ones went into a plastic bin, ones with bad spots were piled on the table to be trimmed. When the bin was full, it was placed on a beam scale and weighed; each was about 50 pounds. 150 pounds would fill the press.

Next the apples in the bin were fed into John's homemade grinder. It was a plywood box with a hinged lid. The box had no bottom; instead there was a rotating wood cylinder with nails driven all around it. The flat nail heads were left about ¼ inch above the surface of the cylinder. The cylinder was driven by a belt connected to an electric motor. Apples were fed into the top of the box, and ground apples fell out the bottom, into a plastic bin.

We used scoops to fill the apple press from the bins of ground apples. The press was simple. Although this one was over 100 years old, modern presses hadn't changed much. The ground apples were piled in a cylinder ringed with vertical boards with gaps between them, held together by steel hoops. The cylinder's bottom was a piece of cast iron with a circular trough all the way around its edge to catch the juice, and a spout at one end. A five gallon plastic jug with a funnel and a wire mesh filter cup was placed below the spout. A threaded rod ran up the middle of the cylinder from the cast iron bottom to six inches above the top of the ring of boards. When the cylinder was full of apples, two thick semicircular boards were placed on top to close the cylinder, a ratcheting threaded steel collar was screwed down the rod until it was tight to the top of the boards, and a long pipe handle was fitted to a hole in the collar.

Then the pressing would begin. Slowly, pressure was applied to the apples by walking the pipe handle around the press, rotating the steel collar down the threads. At first the juice flowed down the cylinder's boards and gushed out of the spout. As the pressing continued, the volume of juice per turn of the press slowed. Eventually the collar needed to be backed off enough to insert spacer boards between it and the bottom boards, so pressing could continue down further. Every few turns the operator stopped to let the juice run out of the press, relieving some of the pressure. Soon the handle would become difficult to turn. The press was spiked into the ground to keep it from tipping over when the handle was pushed hard.

At the end of the press, we left the remaining apples under pressure for twenty minutes or so to let all the juice drip out. By that time we had filled two five gallon jugs. It took the four of us three hours to press 23 gallons of cider. The mash remaining in the press was fed to the sheep and cattle.

Apple cider bought at the supermarket doesn't hold a candle to the cider we pressed at John's house, nor any homemade cider for that matter. Technically, both were apple juice, not cider. Cider is juice that has been fermented. And the best difference was that John's apple juice could be fermented.

Almost all apple juice bought at the supermarket or farm stand is pasteurized to kill bacteria, and has preservatives in it. John's had neither. In fact, if we did nothing to it but let it sit in the jug for a week or two, it would start to harden into alcoholic cider as the yeast present on the apples started their fermentation. This was the type of cider I remembered from my childhood; crisp and fizzy with a small alcohol content. Some folks still did just that: let it sit with the cap loose on the jug for a few months to allow the yeast to do its work, then bottled and aged it to drink the next year. At the end of the fermentation, the alcohol content of the cider would be 6-8%, comparable to that of beer.

Most folks today, however, like to control the process a bit more by adding packaged yeast to the juice, along with some nutrients for the yeast to help ensure it completes its work; turning all the sugars in the juice into alcohol. The problem with the old way - letting the yeast on the apple do the work - was that the final product was unpredictable. The yeast worked slowly so there was more room for molds or bacteria to survive in the juice and overtake the yeast. Or vinegar bacteria might be present, which would eventually spoil the batch (unless apple cider vinegar was what you were after).

After a celebratory bottle of last year's cider in John and Karen's dining room, Keith and I returned home with ten gallons each to ferment, and three gallons to drink right away as apple juice. The cider bubbled away in our basement wine room - along with the elderberry and pumpkin wine - for the next few months, until I bottled it in January. I added brown sugar to the dry cider just before bottling it, and bottled it in beer bottles with crimped caps. The residual yeast consumed the sugar in the weeks after the bottles were sealed, priming them with carbon dioxide. The result was sparkling cider, best when aged until next year's apple crop was ready.

On the day we pressed cider, John remarked that in three hours, were had made $1,500 worth of cider. There were five 750ml bottles of cider per gallon, or 100 bottles in twenty gallons. At the going price of $15 per bottle for aged cider, this equaled $1,500.

That fall, he and Karen pressed 130 gallons, or almost $10,000 worth of cider.

John and I knew the economics of homesteading. He and Karen had taken the same leap that Hilarie and I had when I left architecture. He had read our farm manifesto and remarked he would have written the same thing. We knew stepping off modern life's treadmill was about making do with what you have and finding creative solutions to make what you need, rather than paying someone else to do it for you. It was about minimizing expenses as much as creating income. Our riches came from the places in which we lived. This seldom needed to be measured in cash. We looked in our wine cellars and freezers, at the firewood stacked in our barns, at our gardens and fields and the livestock in them, and measured our independence by their contents. We looked toward our friends who were doing the same, and measured our success by how much abundance we could share with our communities. Hilarie and I would be especially appreciating John's and Karen's overabundance of apple cider.

Nineteen

I used to mark the end of summer with Labor Day weekend and the New York state fair. This year I hadn't the time to make any arbitrary line between the seasons; life on the farm flowed according to the weather and temperature rather than the calendar.

August flowed into September and the kids went back to school; our youngest, Henry, started kindergarten. With all three kids in school and me at home, Hilarie and I had weekdays to ourselves for the first time since we met twenty years ago. Morning and afternoon chores continued as they had all summer; we still had broiler chickens and turkeys in the pasture, still had layers and pigs to take care of. We continued to go to market two days each week; we still butchered on Wednesdays to bring fresh to market every week. And we still had a pile of projects to complete before winter came.

We'd taken a gamble on good fall weather, putting

our last batches of broilers on pasture to be ready in mid-November. October and November in upstate New York could go either way; sometimes we had long Indian summers, and sometimes it snowed by Halloween. One consequence of our gamble was that our preparations for winter were running late as we continued to be busy with our livestock.

Everyone in touch with the land in temperate climates marks two dates every year: last frost and first frost. Our last frost of the previous spring was on May 27th, later than I ever remember it occurring (and two days later we had a stretch of 90 degree weather). Our first frost was on September 17th; about average. The first frost took out our remaining tomatoes and some of the herbs. Salad greens kept chugging along, although growing more slowly in the fall weather. I liked fall greens best for their deep green color and dense flavor.

As fall arrived, things flew by quickly. We were as busy with the farm as we had ever been. On September 24th, we started the wood stove for the first time, beginning our eight month heating season. October was spent doing daily chores, butchering broiler chickens weekly and butchering two flocks of turkeys at the beginning and end of the month. We bottled last May's dandelion wine, started fermenting elderberry and pumpkin wine, and cleaned walnuts.

October 26th marked the last outdoor farmers market in Homer. During October, the number of vendors had dwindled from the usual 25, down to six on the last day. There were probably about as many customers. Produce had shrunk to winter squashes and hoop house greens. The cold and windy weather fit the spirit of the day. Vendors' tents blew down; I had to stand at the front of my tent and hold its edge.

The Homer market would continue indoors once each month from November until April. The winter market scene in the Finger Lakes was growing as more people realized some local farm products were available year round: meats, honey, baked goods, soap and other sundries, crafts, and remaining stocks of winter squash and some hardy greens. We were glad for that; going into the winter we had more stock in our freezers than ever as we prepared to offer pastured meats throughout the year.

By the end of October, our gardens were finished for the year. I cut down the remaining plants and tilled everything under. The garden, as always, had become a burden to me during late summer, and thankfully Hilarie took over most of its harvesting. But as I walked back and forth, guiding the tiller through the beds, I began to think how we would improve the garden for next year: we would spread more compost from the 2 year old pile of horse manure Dad had trucked in for us, and the year after we would spread rich compost from this year's chicken butchering offal mixed with free wood mulch from the town. Next year we would try pinning down weed blocking fabric to reduce labor and warm the soil earlier. There were always new methods and vegetables to test.

The last farmers market at Triphammer was on November first. It had moved inside to the mall's small atrium, and would continue there until the end of November. But again, vendors and customers had dwindled to the point where it no longer made sense to attend.

I was relieved by the end of the markets; the time felt right. There was no sadness for me in the year's endings. Fall is naturally a time of transition. Whereas in my past life Labor Day seemed an abrupt and artificial end to fair weather activities, the farm's gentle, slow transition into fall and winter was natural. Besides, we still had a lot to keep us busy, and the end of the markets freed up the better part of two days each week for work at home.

A morning and evening check of the National Weather Service was part of my routine. On the evening of November eighth I looked at the weather report: sustained 25 degree weather and snow trailed through the forecast from November 12th onward. It was time to get the last of the broiler chickens in. Over the next three days we butchered the last 70 chickens, and November 12th arrived with a big change in weather, as forecasted. We had won our gamble and gotten our late birds in. We took a breath and looked around: what was left? We were carrying our layers and heritage turkeys through the winter. But there were also...the pigs. During the height of summer we had up to 500 animals to care for. Of these, just 3 were not fowl: the pigs. The pigs were easy to forget in their out-of-the-way pasture behind the barn.

We picked them up as piglets in McGraw, which was a half hour's drive away, last April. The breeder kept about twenty sows in separate pens on the lower level of an old barn built into the side of a hill. It was a dim space filled with dust covered cobwebs and lined by fieldstone walls. It reminded me of our old bank barn, demolished when I was a kid. The sows were huge, easily 500 pounds each, and about half of them were nursing piglets. Their owner told us they were all purebred Spotted Durocks. I didn't know anything about pig breeds, but they seemed alright to me, and I was assured by the breeders' list of the other farms he sold his stock to.

We had prearranged a month earlier to have "the pick of the litter;" first choice of a particular sow's piglets. We picked out three: two barrows (castrated males) and one gilt (female). Males were supposed to gain weight a little faster. The gilt had been implanted with a time release birth control capsule which would last five years; the breeder explained he had had problems with other farms inbreeding from his stock. He climbed into the pen and separated the piglets from the sow with a partition (he was braver than I was). As we picked each out, he caught one of their hind legs and lifted them up squealing into the upturned dog crate we had brought to transport them.

They all fit in the dog crate easily, settling in side by side and nose to tail. I noticed later on they would often sleep this way; nose to tail. They were each about 25 pounds, and the breeder and I easily lifted the crate into the back of the truck. I asked him when they would be ready for butchering and he replied, "Umm, along about deer season." Good enough.

Hilarie and I brought them home and put the dog

crate into the three sided shelter I had built in back of
the pole barn. The shelter was on locust post skids, so
I could tow it around. But these three pigs would
spend the rest of their lives with their home in this
pasture, a sort of hog heaven; a fenced rectangle
behind the barn that was filled with brambles, black
walnut trees, some old equipment, and a good sized
piece of sunlit pasture grasses.

Over the summer I fed them twice a day, a total of
over 3,000 pounds from the feed mill plus the large
pasture they turned over inch by inch eating roots,
grubs, worms, and a fair amount of dirt I think. By
the fall they were even crunching black walnuts in
their mouths, which must have been about as hard to
break as stones.

I was not a big fan of the pigs. They didn't fit in
with the rest of the animals on the farm, tucked away
in their pasture behind the barn. While the turkeys,
broiler chickens, and laying chickens did their
organized dance across the pasture in their pens,
eating the grasses and building good soil with their
droppings, the pigs tore up everything within reach.
They were natural bulldozers, but besides a few small
brushy areas, I really didn't need anything on the farm
bulldozed. I was committed to only raising livestock
that could forage part or all their own food, but I
could not raise pigs two years in a row on the same
pasture; they had to be moved, and something had to
be done with the mess they left behind. My parents
loved to see the pigs and frequently brought leftovers
to feed them, and visitors always wanted to see "our
crazy pigs." I often mumbled something about how

their destructive behavior reminded me of too many people I'd met.

I also didn't like the complication of raising pigs. We had control of our poultry from their first day of life all the way through their sale to the customer. I felt details made all the difference at every step, including how they were butchered. But it was illegal for me to butcher the pigs and sell the meat; it had to be done by a facility with a USDA inspector.

And for some reason, I was having trouble pre-selling the meat. When I bought the pigs, I thought I could sell at least two of them as half or whole dressed pigs; an arrangement where we deliver the pigs to the butcher, the butcher determines their dressed weight (without entrails), and the customer pays us a pre-determined dollar per pound for it. Then, the customer pays the butcher directly to have the meat cut as they wish. It seemed I could sell poultry all day long, but pork buyers were few and far between. For the entire summer, I managed to pre-sell only ½ of one pig. In hindsight, I think few people have dedicated freezers like they used to, and most people prefer to buy cuts as they need them.

In November, by my amateur guess, the pigs had grown to each weigh over 250 pounds. It was time for them to go to the butcher. Anyone living in the country will tell you a good butcher is hard to find, and most will disagree about the merits of each. Over the summer, I talked to other vendors at the farmers markets, and finally decided our pigs would go to Owasco Meats in Moravia, my parents' butcher of choice since I was a kid. Being that butchers book months in advance, in July I made my reservation: November 12th.

In October, I went to see the nice ladies in the old house trailer that served as Owasco Meats' office to discuss how the pigs would be cut: pork chops or loin roasts? Hot, mild, or sweet sausage? Hams, bacon, pork steaks? Small world; that same old house trailer was the one I grew up in, next door to our farm before my parents built their house. Upon hearing this, the two ladies - who were mother and daughter - expressed their amazement and happily gave me a tour of the old place. My bedroom hadn't changed a bit since I was seven years old in 1975 (the last time I had seen it), except it was piled high with boxes.

Before I left I asked them for a recommendation on a hauler to get the pigs from the farm to the butcher. They gave me no names. *I learned that haulers also book months in advance.* Crap. Luckily, our neighbor with the organic dairy and beef farm, Eileen Scheffler recommended a hauler named John, who agreed to squeeze us into his busy schedule. He told me how much he cared for the little guys in farming (us!). I felt lucky.

We seemed to have everything organized. That feeling lasted until the afternoon of November 12th. Coincidentally (and probably a harbinger of events to come), this was the very same day that the weather took a steep change for the worse; the day after Hilarie and I finished butchering our last broiler chickens.

On the morning of the November 12th, John, my hauler had a busy day in front of him, moving dozens of cows from this farm to that, back and forth. The evening before, he assured me over the phone he would be at my place around 3:30pm. Good: that gave us 1½ hours of light. I knew little about moving pigs, but I did know their eyesight isn't very good, and they tend to hunker down when it gets dark.

I was a little worried by the time John showed up at 4:30, with a 30' long rig that could hold 100 pigs. Good thing he had brought the smaller rig, with the new admission he had never hauled pigs before, and in snow that was falling harder and harder, and with a steep hill to get up on the way to the butcher. Still, I tried to remain confident. I had a bucket full of apples, the pigs' favorite treat. They always followed me when I had food. "This should be easy" I thought.

John backed his huge trailer to the pig pasture's gate at the corner of the barn, wiping out only one nice ten year old lilac bush, and taking only about 20 minutes to do so as he navigated our back lawn, which resembles a miniature golf course in terms of obstacles and winding fairways.

At this point it was getting dark. The pigs looked at us from their shelter; they were settling in for the night. A little voice was telling me we were screwed. But I still had my ace in the hole: my bucketful of apples for pigs that had not eaten since early morning.

John finally got his trailer lined up and we opened the pasture gate. I went in with my apples; fed the pigs from my hand; led them to the gate. They would not cross the fence line. Although pigs have poor eyesight, they have a good memory of where the electric fence's zap line is. They would not cross the

247

line, apples or not. We couldn't get behind them and herd them in; that would excite them and we'd surely be done.

Actually, we were done. It was now 6pm, dark, and John had to get home to milk his own 50 cows. I appreciated John's efforts even though we were not successful, but he refused to take any money for his time. He recommended a fellow hauler named Stuart, who had a smaller rig, to come back tomorrow morning and try again. At 7pm I called the butcher and confirmed: if we could get the pigs to his place by 9am the next morning we would not lose our place in line. If we didn't, their next opening was in January. January would NOT work.

Stuart, the new hauler, turned out to be an old family acquaintance. I called him up right away after calling the butcher. Yes, he could be here first thing in the morning, and in fact, he could come over tonight and take a look at our setup to see how best to do the loading. In a half hour his truck headlights were shining on the pasture gate and he was telling me what I should do: take the feed trough out of the pasture. At first light, build a 16' long chute to the gate with plywood. Feed the pigs at the gate end of the chute and close the back end. Open the gate with the truck parked in front. Use straw bales to wall the gap between the truck and the fence, and to create a step up to the trailer bed. I thanked Stuart, and swore I'd never raise pigs again. "You'll change your mind about that." he said, and left.

I went to Keith's house to visit, and he agreed to help me get things set up the next morning. I didn't sleep much that night.

The next morning, I went out to the pigs' pasture at 5:30. It was still cold; the pasture was covered with snow and frozen crusty mud. The sun was dim in the east among clouds. After a quick breakfast, I was out scrounging materials to make a chute. I had plenty of metal fence posts to support the walls, and a bunch of old doors to make the walls from. Stuart said it was important that the pigs not be able to see through the barrier. Otherwise they would test it, and there was little that would stop them. I hammered the posts into the ground and wired the doors to them; solid enough. Keith came at 7am and we looked at the chute. Stuart was to be there at 8am. Everything looked good, so Keith left to tend to his mare with an injured hoof, and I waited in the heated workshop. I was sure the pigs were leaving one way or the other today; you can guess the other.

At 7:30 Keith came back and we began our one chance. I really felt it was one chance: if we spooked the pigs they would only be leaving the "other" way. I filled the pigs' feeder trough with grain and some apples, and placed it inside the newly-made chute near the gate. One pig wandered in, then two. The third was more interested in Keith, who was standing near the chute end, in the pasture. Keith took some apples and led the last pig into the chute with quiet words of encouragement. Who knew; Keith was a pig whisperer! I shut the enclosure with the last old door. We high-fived and waited ten minutes until the hauler backed in. The pigs were eating their assorted delicacies, hungry from a day without food. I couldn't remember the last time I felt as satisfied as having those three pigs in that 4'x16' chute, eating contentedly.

More reinforcements came with Stuart: his buddy, Tom, rode shotgun, and our next door neighbor, Dan Starner, came too. We stacked some straw bales between the trailer and the gate, and broke a bale and used its pieces as a step up into the trailer. Keith and I used a piece of plywood to gradually push the pigs down the chute...and up into the trailer! Mission accomplished!

I paid Stuart and he pulled out of the driveway. I called the butcher and happily let him know our pigs would be there on time...then Dad and I went downtown to purchase a new chest freezer for all the pork that would be coming back to us in a few weeks. I was grateful to have met two haulers who cared about the little guy, and for our neighbors' help.

That day - November 13th - made a line in our calendar. It was the day we shut the farm down for the winter. Suddenly, everything seemed quiet. A few days later, I finished putting away all the equipment; parking the pasture pens together for the winter and putting the fencing, feeders, and waterers away. Chores, which consisted of opening and closing the turkey and laying hen houses, gathering eggs, and feeding and watering, now needed to be done only once each day, and took only a half hour.

On November 16th deer season began. I shot two deer on opening day, which Keith and I butchered and had in the freezer a few days later. The weather turned consistently cold, and I hunted only a handful of days after that.

A few days after Stuart hauled our pigs away, Owasco Meats called and happily reported our pigs were the nicest they had seen this season, and they had dressed large, between 250 and 275 pounds. Typically pigs of that age dressed around 200 pounds. I wasn't sure whether the butcher's statements about quality were true or just flattery, or whether their happiness about the hanging weights meant fatty pigs and profit for them, or leaner meat and more back for us. But I didn't worry too much about all this, and eagerly awaited our pork, especially the smoked cuts.

We had all our pork back from the butcher by mid-December. The smoked pork (hams and bacon) took a few weeks longer than the rest. They were worth the wait; smoked the old fashioned way, with time. Hilarie and I tried each type of cut, meal by meal, over the next weeks. Our pigs were delicious, and our customers agreed. The cuts flew out of the freezer in $100 multiples. My worries over selling pork ended.

With December came more cold and snow, and not a thaw in sight. The farm turned inward. Since November and the end of the markets, customers had been coming a few days each week to pick up their holiday turkeys and other meat. I delivered chicken, eggs, and pork to our regular customers when I could combine those trips with other errands.

We settled into winter's quiet, and celebrated a successful first season on the farm. I think we will raise pigs next year.

Twenty

December's bite was hard this year, and she held it long. During the entire month, there were only a few days above freezing. Hilarie and I settled into our new winter routine and watched the woodpile shrink alarmingly fast.

It was natural to slow down; I talked to my farmer friends and found they now had time to read or watch television some afternoons. We could visit with them, talking for a few hours, passing the time in front of the stove. The day's activities were dependent on the weather. If it was sunny and not windy, we could work outside in twenty degree temperatures. Keith and I took walks in the woods for exercise. Just as December's cold balanced the uncommonly warm fall, so its hibernation time balanced the 16 hour workdays of summer.

I read, wrote, and cracked walnuts. I went to matinees on weekday afternoons. I caught up with the doings of our customers when they stopped by the farm to pick up chickens, eggs, and pork. I watched the birds at the feeder while writing at the dining room table.

Once a month I went to the Homer winter market, held in the garage of a former car dealership. There was no heat and we stamped our feet on the cold concrete floor. There were never more than ten vendors there. I did a brisk business as regular customers stocked up on a month's worth of meat. It was nice to see old friends from the summer.

Christmas and the New Year came and went. I can't remember enjoying time spent with family over the holidays as much as this year. I had time: time to relax, time to be present.

On January 7th, eleven months to the day after leaving, I returned for the first time to the office where I had worked. It was a lark, really. I needed my laptop fixed and Aaron, the firm's IT person met me in Cortland for lunch to take care of the problem. It turned out he needed to connect it to the office's network to do the repairs, so I rode up with him and arranged a ride back to Cortland at the end of the day with Deborah Rhea.

I stepped off the elevator and into the office, and was warmly greeted by my old coworkers. To an outsider, I would have seemed quite out of place there, with my long hair and beard, jeans and flannel shirt. My appearance was a source of conversation; it had been all through the preceding year as one by one, folks from the office visited the farm and gave their opinions.

I made my way around the office, catching up with people. Eventually I was standing in front of my old desk.

There he was, still sitting there: my old self. I looked down at him, but he did not look up at me. He was staring at his computer screen and clicking his mouse. He would not be disturbed. I felt for him. I had left a ghost of myself in this place; an old me I no longer understood. Why did he wait so long to do what I did? Why had he been afraid? I was sad for him and embarrassed by his presence. I wanted him to disappear, but there he was, skulking at his desk. He was not me.

The imprint of this experience remained with me after I returned home and in dark January's ruminations. It came into my dreams.

*   *   *

I returned to the mansion by way of a lane through the woods, which wound along the side of a small lake. The lane ended at the mansion's grounds on the lake. I parked my car amongst many others in the lot and walked inside. Downstairs it was quiet, but I heard mumbled speech above.

I climbed the stairs and stepped into a warehouse-type room. It was like an old factory, with wood columns and floors. The ceilings had exposed wood beams. It was very large but I could not see its boundaries because it was filled with objects. These were the same wonderful things I had seen on my previous trips to the mansion, but the small rooms and hallways had disappeared, made into this one

255

large room. The objects were too many to understand, like arriving at a library and seeing many books but no particular title. They were arranged with winding paths between piles, and as I walked toward the source of the speech I had heard, I began to notice singular objects along the way: here was an egg scale, and a stack of china, and here was a large intricate bar removed from an old pub, and a mirror with an ornate frame.

As I walked, I met people who were carrying things toward the stairs. Then, I arrived at the source of the noise: an auctioneer and a crowd. The mansion was being emptied. I entered the crowd and asked a man what had happened. "The widow died," he said, "and everything is being sold."

I stayed with the crowd and bought some things, but eventually the crowd shuffled past me as the auctioneer kept moving toward the next objects for sale. I watched buyers picking up their purchases and carrying them back toward the stairs. As I stood in place, the room gradually cleared. I could see it was not one large room, but rather many partially enclosed rooms, such that I could still not understand the mansion as a whole, could not understand its entire size or shape.

I meandered through the empty spaces. The auctioneer's voice faded as we moved farther apart. By chance, I found a large glassed-in porch which faced the lake. The lake's surface was flat and dark, a mystery. I looked up and looked down through the roof and floor, saw the lawn below and the sky above, and realized the extent of the mansion's disrepair.

Who cared to repair things like the mansion these days? It would probably be torn down, and this may be my last visit.

The caretaker found me and showed me the way to the roof, where his equipment and his quarters were. His job was to take care of the building, but it had become too much for him to keep up. We walked across the flat roof and into a small penthouse. The penthouse was not entirely enclosed; parts of its walls were bed sheets and tarps hung from clotheslines. They waved in the breeze.

The penthouse contained heating and ventilation equipment, and sparse accommodations for the caretaker: a small bed, nightstand, and sink. Arranged on top of and alongside the equipment, all around, was the caretakers own collection. He had brought me here to show me it. "This is the best of the best." he said. "I've been in the mansion my whole life, and brought its most special objects up here. The widow never missed them. She hasn't been upstairs in decades." He was a twitchy little man. "I'm staying up here with it, no matter what becomes of the mansion." I pictured him standing in his little penthouse, falling, as the mansion eventually caved in to ruins.

On my way back to my car, I stopped at a cottage on the mansion's grounds. There was a van parked outside. The cottage was long and narrow, a single story with open porches on all four sides. Standing inside the porch, I could see this was a house that belonged in the tropics. It was not a part of this place; it looked nothing like the Victorian mansion and could not survive a cold winter. It had no outside walls; it was just a ring of ground level porches surrounding a raised floor, covered by a log-framed thatched roof.

"The medium is not at home," said one of the workmen in coveralls, "but you can wait if you'd like. We have to get everything that could blow away out of here." They were busy moving all the house's smaller contents; photos, dishware, and knick-knacks, into the van. Another group of men was pouring concrete around the bottom of the furniture that remained, and around a nondescript refrigerator-sized stainless steel cabinet in the living area.

"You can put anything you'd like to keep into the cabinet." I heard the medium's voice but she was not there. I opened the cabinet but someone had already decided what I should have in it; its shelves were full. I seated myself on a couch. From here, I could look out over the lake and around the mansion's grounds. I could see parts of the mansion, but other parts were a mystery, tucked into the woods. I waited for the medium's return. Eventually I fell asleep.

I woke to dim, low sunlight revealing the morning's ruin. I still sat on the couch, and the rest of the furniture still sat on the cottage's rectangular raised floor, locked into place by the concrete poured by the workmen. But everything else was broken, shattered, or gone; I guess it had been blown away by a great storm in the night. The cottage's structure, except the floor, had disappeared. Broken pieces of wood and loose papers were everywhere. All the workmen and auction people were gone. The mansion lay in a great collapsed heap. The lake was as still as ever.

The cabinet, dented, still stood. Its doors faced me as I sat on the couch. I rose and opened the doors. Its contents were still safe inside.

-blink-

Grandpa had a friend in Ithaca named George Parkens, who was very old. We visited him occasionally. We sat at his large dining room table, which was piled with stuff, in the middle of his large stuff-cluttered house. Grandpa sat and talked with George, and I wandered the lower story of the house, looking at all the old things. Once in a while I could hear the ring of George's spit hitting the brass spittoon on the floor beside him. He carried it wherever he went.

-blink-

After Grandpa died I was scared of his empty house. I wouldn't go inside alone. Dad had left the electricity on and sometimes, from my parents house in the evening, we could see the living room light was on. Dad went over in the darkness to pull the light's chain, turning it off.

-blink-

January's world imploded: bed, kitchen, and dining

room. My old self slammed into my new self. He screamed. I'd wasted my education, given up my success, and turned my back on my potential. What would I be in ten years? What about my family, my children? He was so afraid and he made me feel the same.

And what about you? How did you live? What did you care about? I asked him and he shrank back into his corner. You defined yourself by what others thought. You signed a contract to bury who you were to become what convention wanted you to be, with shallow measures of success as your payment. What about your family? You were gone all the time. And worst of all, you knew you made the wrong decision long ago, but you buried it, and you made me hurt for so long. I was there. I was the voice deep inside you that cried out.

And you almost won, didn't you? I almost gave into you; I almost let you take control again last summer. You would have had me back in that life as if nothing had ever happened. I'm standing on my own now. I don't need anyone to validate me. Leave, I don't want you here with me.

Twenty-One

Or *and* **and.**

Nothing exists within the **or.** *It is geometry's line without thickness.*
The **or** *is duality; it is two: two entities with no relationship.*
Much can exist within the **and.** *It is the fertile width of recombination.*

*

Any relationship exists in the space of **and.** *You* **and** *I.*
You and I is a triad: you, I, **and:** *the relationship. Three distinct parts*
There are two primary colors of relationship: mediation and reconciliation
Their difference lies in the consciousness, or lack thereof, of the **and.**

*

*Assume you and I are opposites; poles (+) and (-).
Our entry into a relationship can either preserve the oppositeness
of the poles or can seek, in degree, to homogenize the poles.
Mediation compromises the poles. Reconciliation preserves the
poles.*

*Mediation changes each of the two poles. Mediation is
algorithmic, without consciousness, an average. A narrowing of
the spectrum between poles toward synthesis.*

*Reconciliation preserves the poles via a consciousness residing in
the reconciliator. This consciousness is lent by each of the poles
as a lace child, with its own emergent properties. Reconciliation
preserves the width of the spectrum between poles, and the poles
may remain pure.*

*The reconciliator completes a triad of three conscious entities:
you, I, and the reconciliatory relationship. You and I change
and become through time. The reconciliator must always be
becoming; it must improvisationally evolve the relationship of
unyielding poles through time's change.*

-"Triads" January 2013

*   *   *

In my old life, I met a man named Mel Toomey. I
was introduced to Mel through a mutual
acquaintance. He read my essays and he saw I was
doing original thinking. He invited me to spend three
262

days at his lakefront house in Connecticut.

The lake and house were beautiful. Mel had purchased the entire lake and its surrounding forest from a timber company a few decades ago. He subdivided the land and sold the pieces for the construction of houses. The largest and best lot he saved for himself. His house projected from the hillside just above the lake. It was modern, tastefully and minimally furnished. It had an indoor lap pool adjacent to the living room, a full workout room, and a guest suite. Everything looked toward the lake with floor to ceiling windows. The lake was surrounded by trees, offering little evidence of the other houses around it.

Mel had founded an intensive leadership program that graduated two classes per year. But he was by no means the cheap suit, white teeth bullshitting glad-hander cliché of the leadership business. He had been working for years on a "language to express ideas," as he called it, and his thinking was infused with Eastern influences. He had a quiet strength. Before his retirement, he built a successful leadership consulting business in New Jersey. Every morning, a personal chauffer had driven him from his home in northwestern Connecticut to work and back.

On our first evening, Mel took me to dinner in town. We talked about view and centricity. View, Mel explained, was concerned with distance and detail. He used a tall lifeguard stand on an ocean beach as an example. Standing on the ground, one couldn't see far out into the water, but one could see things close by in great detail: the eye color of passersby and the type of shells on the beach, for example. From the seat at the top of the stand, the view changed. One could see further out in the water, but the further one saw, the less detail was visible and the more uncertain one became of what they were seeing. And the details of the beach could no longer be seen; eye colors, shells, etc.

Centricity was the place one most favored to occupy. Following the life guard example, some may prefer to stand high on the structure and see great distances, and others may prefer, in degree, to stand lower and lower on its ladder, all the way down to the beach. Each place along the ladder had its own merits, its own particular combination of distance, clarity, and detail.

Mel taught me healthy businesses and communities were comprised of individuals all along the ladder. Complementary views were needed to give the business or community the most clarity of vision. Centricity applied to all sorts of spectra. It applied to time; people could be past-, present-, and future-centric. Some may find comfort in replicating what was successful for them in the past, others may be more inclined to try new and different things. Centricity also applied to practicality and abstraction. Some preferred to talk about the things they could lay their hands on; they liked to read "how-to" books and things grounded in science and measurability. Others liked to think of what "could be;" preferred working in undefined, blurry, or emotion-based territory. They were concerned with things that were difficult to measure, such as meaning and happiness. Each of us occupied a particular bandwidth on the spectrum. Some had narrow ranges of view and centricity, and others wide.

Mel and I spent the next two days exploring dualities. It may seem like a long time to talk about such a thing, but we looked at dualities through many lenses. The subject deserved the time we spent on it, because the solutions to many of our collective troubles, and the further development of my work in architecture, would depend on moving past dualistic thinking.

Mel explained what a duality was with a few examples. One was two neighboring planets and a satellite. The satellite could orbit one planet or the other, but not both. It could only be "continuously falling" (that is what an orbit is), toward one planet at once. Another example was an electric charge. Molecules were either charged (+) or (-); they either had more electrons than protons or not.

Mel's most powerful example lay in two words: "or" and "and." "Or" was a symptom of dualistic thought. It excluded one condition for the other, created poles (+) and (-), and allowed no complex relationship or middle ground between the two. "And" allowed combinations of the poles along a spectrum. Black "and" white made many grays. Black "or" white put things into only two groups, and implied there was no gray between.

Dualistic thinking disrupted relationships. "One side or the other" implied each side was whole in itself; that it did not need the other. "One side and the other" implied both sides and their relationship made a whole. Despite what political pundits espoused, most people were combinations of "ands;" they did not fall neatly into narrow party platforms. Following our discussion of view and centricity, any healthy group needed participants from all along a spectrum.

There were wide applications for the work Mel and I did. It applied to understanding healthy political discourse with respect for multiple viewpoints. The same applied to businesses and communities. I began to understand how to better work with large and diverse community groups on projects. It centered on creating an inclusive vision, and on enabling every person to express their agenda in the finished result, be it a building or a business plan. I learned to see, after Mel's concepts, people's view, centricity, and bandwidth. Once I knew this, I knew how far they could be pulled. Nobody would travel too far outside of their bandwidth at a given time, but over time, folks could be gradually pulled further and further into new territory. Mel called this cantilevering. I called it stretching the rubber band.

In the years following my visit with Mel, I continued to think about and work on the subject of dualities. One day I crossed it with a general exploration of the nature of relationships, and let both simmer together. I believed healthy relationships were the key to just about everything I had been working on in sustainability and architecture: We needed to establish healthy relationships between people, the things they made (technology), and their environment. A marriage, following my earlier analogy. I shifted my focus from talking about technology and nature dualistically, and began to treat nature as a oneness that included us, our technology, and our environment.

Dualism implied two entities with no relationship. The relationship made all the difference. I saw the relationship between two as a triad: the first entity, the second entity, and their relationship. The relationship, although often invisible and difficult to quantify, especially in the case of human relationships, was just as important as the two others in the triad. In fact, I felt that in the most complex relationships, each entity lent a piece of their consciousness to the relationship, so that the relationship itself became its own consciousness, born of the combined consciousnesses of its two entity-parents. These complex relationships I called lace children.

I first developed the concept of lace children earlier in my career, when I was immersed in putting together buildings. Architects create thousands of detailed drawings to describe the construction of a large building. As I spent months drawing the building's parts and how they fit together, brick by brick and beam by beam, the creation began to take on a simple consciousness of its own; it began to tell me what it wanted to be, to draw itself. I had lent enough of my consciousness to the endeavor that part of it spun off and lived of itself. Then my relationship with it became an interaction, and I rushed to put on paper what it told me about itself, finishing the building's drawings. I felt I was not the only parent of the lace child, that there was some energy giving it life

267

and a living environment while my attention was elsewhere. This second parent I called the fabric, the unifying energy that lays beneath all things; the source of spirituality.

The lace child relationship, having a simple consciousness born of its two parents, had the ability to reconcile their differences. That is, both individuals were able to maintain their uniqueness and have a healthy and ever-evolving relationship. The creation of the lace child required considerable investment on the part of each of the parents, the "married couple" as it were. But once it was born, the relationship "became" with its parents. As they grew and changed, the lace child relationship did as well. The relationship remained healthy because it was intelligent, dynamic, and did not compromise the identity of either participant.

The essay that leads this chapter was written just before I left architecture, and, along with the control and vision concepts described earlier, formed a complete final version of the philosophy I had worked on during the four years preceding. In hindsight, it was the proper time to move on to new explorations.

*　　*　　*

The old self I had found at the office wouldn't leave me alone. He visited me those long January nights and I wrestled with his fear. He would not be ignored.

One day I relented, understanding he had to be

acknowledged and embraced. I could no more cut him away than my own arm; he was a part of me, and he had important things to say. He and I were two parts of the same self in a relationship. After all, I could not be who I was without his enduring what he went through. He provided the financial security from which I took my leaps. He had suffered long for my freedom, and I loved him.

His view and centricity were different than mine. He flew high and I flew low. He had spent most of his later years near the top of the lifeguard stand, working first in the abstractions of design philosophy, then climbing down to manage the practical considerations of its implementations only when necessary. I, on the other hand, had become concerned with what was right in front of my face, observing the details of the farm and taking satisfaction in the meditative routine of hands-dirty labor. But weren't these complements of a single whole? I cared about, wrote about, the full spectrum. I cared not for a sole focus on the concrete, cared not for a steady diet of "how-to" books on farming. And I cared not for the unceasing, untethered flights of abstraction that philosophical development could pull me along on. I cared for both, together.

He and I, the man I saw in the chair at work and my present self, reconciled our relationship to form a healthy triad. Outwardly we may seem like a whole, a singular person. But within, it is he, I, and our ever-becoming relationship. I listen to and reassure his fears. He gives me access to his unending well of ideas; his philosophical ruminations. We are brothers.

Twenty-Two

I can't stop thinking now.

Now now now now now now now now now first light to last dark forever my consciousness.

Now impales me smack between my eyes. It's the funny little spot my finger pushes around between my eyebrows. My mind wanders but this convergence of eyes and brows lingers. God drove this rubber stake into my presence right there; it is our mortality. It drags me forever forward, now that slippery devil that's never where you left it. Stretching looking into the darkness straining for a vacation into yesterday or tomorrow bungeed snap slapped back now. Ouch. Flicked between the eyes.

NOW! demands, pragmatically taps its forefinger on the table. Damned now always wants me. Now swallows my tomorrows and buries my yesterdays.

We are united now on this one train now now now now now now clickity clack our whole giant world stuffed onto one car rolling down the tracks. Sorry, the doors are locked. Ah, now is not the only car it's one of an endless train and what if I could go to the next car or the car behind; what if my now is five minutes ahead of your now, or five minutes behind? We'd both be there and lost to each other, my prime now out of phase with your prime now. I'm squishing my brows eyes and nose together to make the jump. Nope, never works and now my brain hurts with the implications of phased nows.

And now if I could jump on top of the train and run way back a hundred cars, I could find the now of my great grandfather and ride along for awhile. We'd talk and look out the windows; what scenery his now passed my train car far ahead had passed before me. Still, even in his now, life is now now now now now now down the tracks, will reach the spot where my home car once was. He doesn't but his remains do; the dusty dead world of his now car still riding down the tracks with its lights out.

Now I'm thinking of the flickering frames of an old movie. The projector clacks now now now now now twenty-four frames per second. I'm sitting in the theater blinking my eyes in tune with each frame. I've compartmentalized the flowing now of my train into bitsy little freeze-frame nows. I run upstairs and grab the reel from the projector and let it unroll down the lobby stairs. Each frame a now built from scratch, torn down and rebuilt with just a tiny difference and shot for the next frame; super eight claymation movies made in my childhood.

I should be thankful my forehead ligamented now held while I dream through time. I may pull hard enough one day to drag the stake out of the now, escape time's train and away I'll go rolling down the bank chasing some parallel train never to be seen by mine I love now, my train's lights fading away and me running unleashed into the darkness. I hope someone will take care of the now I left behind.

-"NOW" December 2012

*　　*　　*

Now is February eighth, 2014; one year and one day since I left. I am sitting at our dining room table watching the finches and chickadees at the feeder. They perch in the birch tree and on the arbor's dormant wisteria vines, taking turns flying down to the feeder, getting their sunflower seed, and then returning to their perch to shell and eat it. Once in a while a pair of cardinals shows up and the smaller birds scatter.

The yard outside is bright with sunshine reflected off new snow. This has been one of the coldest winters in recent memory. This morning it was ten degrees when I went outside to open the chicken and turkey houses. The birds don't seem to mind the cold.

I went over to help Keith unthaw the frozen heating pipes in his basement this morning. They had been frozen since yesterday morning, when it dropped to fifteen below. He had space heaters and heat lamps all over the place, trying to find where the pipes froze. I brought over Dad's blasting propane heater and fired it up in Keith's basement. I'm hoping to hear soon from him that his pipes have thawed.

The old clocks are all around me here in the dining room, each ticking their own beat, holding me to NOW. The Seth Thomas wooden-geared grandfather clock ticks slowest, at once per second. The wall clocks tick twice per second, and the mantle clocks four times per second. I am content now, riding the seasons' cycles. Thus my NOW looks more like a merry go round than a train. I am tied to nature's repeating rhythms.

I have changed much in the last 366 days. Sometimes the changes seemed out of my control, as when I no longer cared to watch TV and quit reading. I read again now (thankfully), but I doubt I will ever again enjoy television. I don't care for its messages.

This morning I asked Hilarie what she had noticed most about me during the last year. She said I am closer to her and to our children. I am here at home with them instead of gone 12 hours every day. But she meant more than just that; it was that my presence had changed, that I was content to exist "now," without trying to speed it to tomorrow or next week.

I am thankful to be living in the light of beauty. It is all around me on the farm, in my family, in the places I go. I existed in dark ugliness for too long; on the four lanes and in the cubicles, on the commercial strips and around the giant cold buildings; in the dead places no one nurtured. A part of me went dark for a long time; the quiet little boy with his Grandpa. I am emotional about this: no one should be made to exist in dead places. Beauty happens in the places we let it; nature will provide it if we would only hold our hand away. The dead places are made when we turn our back on nature's principles, and apply artificial value sets to what we create.

The health of our farm glows as if a luminescent fabric had been laid over it. Even today under snow and in the cold, the bright embers of the birds at the feeder, all the cares of the generations of my family in this house, and the pastures hibernating under their blankets warmly glow in my vision. In the spring this place will again erupt in riotous light. Why would I want to be any place or any time else?

Sometimes I will begin a story to someone with, "When I was working..." and I have to catch myself. I used to work as an architect, now I do not work anymore. At least that is the way I see it. Someone looking in from the outside would see that I am working as hard as I ever have, but I still do not feel I am working.

How many times have we heard someone say, "I wish I did not have to go to work today." The word "work" has become synonymous with toil; with tasks we must perform but would rather not. How many people dream of winning the lottery and quitting their jobs? This speaks of the danger of signing society's contract, which puts us on the materialism treadmill. In order to prove our success, we must have more money, stuff, and fame. Dare to jump off.

I may as well call our choice that of "working" and "living." I used to work. Now I live. There is no work life and home life for me; it is all one. The compartmentalization of life caused by different value sets in work and home life is one of the worst products of the rat race. The things we are rewarded for at work we may not be proud of in any other part of our life. "Yeah I really screwed that other guy at work and got the big raise, and then I went home and had to talk to my son about his getting caught cheating in school." I once thought I had to deaden a part of myself to excel at work, and eventually I

275

forgot how to reawaken that part of myself when I arrived home. The result of all this is what (in my work life!) I called cognitive dissonance; a life that felt fragmented and confused.

I exist in synthesis now. There is little distinction between how our family earns its income and how we live. Farming has a wonderful way of becoming your life. I am proud to say I am a farmer; anyone should. Those who associate farming with drudgery and its clichés of poverty and ignorance don't understand what it really is, or are thinking of the industrial version of farming.

What could be more fulfilling than caring for, nurturing, life? What could be more noble? And if our continuing existence on this planet, a sustainable existence, is rooted in our finding a place, calling it ours, and caring for its health as we would our own health, then nothing gets closer to that goal than farming. Our family is a part of this land as much as the grass growing in the pasture. Our health depends on its health.

None of these goals are realized if farming continues to centralize and specialize. The tractor jockey who sows one crop on all his land, the dairy farmer with 5,000 head spraying liquid manure over square miles of land, are products of industrialism's "bigger is better" economic models. Trucking food over thousands of miles, *importing chicken meat from China,* are products of industrialism's artificially cheap energy. This cannot continue; it will collapse under its own weight. Consumers of that system's products are already feeling the nutritional consequences of its short-sightedness and chemical dependency. The land hurts with its chemically fertilized and herbicided exhaustion.

The young people leaving college and entering farming today, like Daniel at the Homer Farmers Market, offer hope. They see farming in its new version as their future. This is a future of farming lightly on the land; working with it instead of ceaselessly plowing its life under and stamping it out with the tractor tire. This is smart farming; there is some drudgery certainly, but the challenge is for each of us to carefully observe nature's interactions happening around us and smartly fit our activities to them, avoiding drudgery whenever possible. This farming is about loving a place and personally knowing those who will eat what you produce, knowing that you are responsible and accountable for its quality. This is farming decentralized. Its seeds are taking root all over this country.

Those who would farm will not feel successful unless they are clear about the relationship of income to their definition of success. I did not become a farmer for the money. Like John McGillen's definition of himself as a homesteader, being creative with what he had and thrifty with what he purchased, our decision to start farming assumed we would either need to create for ourselves, or do without some of the time. The more things we can grow, the cheaper our grocery bill. The more energy we make, the lower our utility bill. The more things we know how to repair, the fewer new things we need to buy, and the fewer mechanics we need to hire. Bringing out the cash is always a last resort.

As a small farmer, I measure success by less quantifiable, yet more important things, than income. Are my children experiencing the rich connection to place that I experienced when I was a child? Are we closer as a family? Am I proud of what I produce? Are my livestock raised humanely? Am I increasing the health of my land for future generations? Am I making a positive contribution to my community? Am I being a responsible global citizen? When I close my accounting books, review these questions, and proudly say "yes" to each of them, I am a success. Be assured, I must depend on income for part of my success, but once the mortgage, credit card, and car payments are gone, and we adopt a make-do attitude, cash becomes a much smaller factor.

During the past one year and one day, I went through the most difficult struggle of my life. I would not wish that on anyone. I questioned who I was and how I would live the rest of my life. The leaps I took were gut-wrenchingly scary at the time; they felt like jumping out of a World War One trench in the midst of machine gun fire. The first six months I was deathly afraid of making the wrong decisions. When the day came that I had to make a choice between my old life in architecture and my new life farming, my head told me one thing and my heart told me another. I tried to satisfy both at first, then learned it was the heart which knew best. I should have known; in my work life, I knew that to convince anyone of the merits of change, I had to appeal to their heart. Once the heart was convinced, the head would follow.

In my heart, our first year on the farm was a success beyond where I ever imagined I would be on the day I left work. In just eight months we developed our farm's ethic, constructed the beginnings of its infrastructure, raised and sold chickens, eggs, turkeys, pork, and walnuts, developed a loyal customer base for our products, and connected with our community.

My quiet afternoons writing at the dining room table are about to come to an end for the season. In two weeks, if the weather cooperates, maple sugaring and sap boiling will begin. Then we will be starting seeds, building new fences, constructing a brooder, buying our first cattle, and putting the chickens back on pasture. Our cycle begins again.

Epilogue

Nature is forever becoming, always changing. There is nothing on this Earth that has not been disturbed by our activities; climax ecosystems knocked down the rungs of the stability ladder. Here in the Northeast, the climax ecosystem hemlock forests had been greatly diminished before the arrival of the Europeans, burned by indigenous peoples to grow crops and clear aisles in the forests to drive big game across for a clear bow shot. Settlers found chestnut, maple, beech, ash and oak forests. Now the chestnuts are long gone, the beeches are succumbing to their own slow blight, and we monitor the advance of the emerald ash borer from the west. Bill McKibben saw the end of nature in 1989; the end of nature unaffected by our activities.

Now, in the Northeast, what we call wild is actually the pastoral; the farm fields and forests bearing the mark of our management. Not quite wild, and not quite a backyard garden, but still managed, still subject to the human hand.

My personal journey, as well as that of many others, is forever becoming. One night Hilarie and I mapped my personal development, and identified "flips" throughout my life, occurring on a four to six year period. These flips always had one thing in common; they moved from a pole of abstract thought to a pole of applied craft, then back. This book tracks one such flip toward applied craft, but informed by the abstract thought occurring before the flip. What comes next? That is exciting. For me, and maybe for you, forever becoming is life, and stasis is death. I like to think of these flips as an upward spiral where one pole informs the other, and each is developed in turn as the spiral winds its way around itself.

Still, many people's development slows down or stops at some time. Their hairstyle freezes on high school graduation day (I'm proud to say I lost my mullet in college), their musical tastes stagnate, or they stop learning how to incorporate new technology into their lives. This world is about accelerating change and is forever becoming. Toward what I know not, but I believe it's a safe guess to say its path includes increasing natural resource scarcity.

Increasing natural resource scarcity will lead us to eventually wake up to the crazy things we do today, and we will reconcile our habits to current solar income. Our government is considering allowing the shipment of chickens to China for processing, which would then be shipped back to the US for consumption. Under what common sense does this fall? It is the product of artificially cheap energy and unfair wage distribution. When I was an architect, I used to ask consultants to imagine the work shown on their drawings being performed without the use of fossil fuels: gasoline and diesel. Regrading a site with shovels and draft animals? Setting structural steel with scaffolding, blocks and tackle, and strong backs? It put the whole endeavor of building into a new light. As it should, I argued, because our cheap energy was a temporary thing; a bank account we were draining that drew no interest and no new principle.

We must learn how to thrive in a world of accelerating change. I see decentralization and resiliency as the primary themes of change. Think of the money and energy we are obligated to spend on large centralized systems: sewer plants, water plants, and miles of pipe; asphalt highways, bridges, food trucked thousands of miles, electricity 30% efficient from central plants belching waste and long distribution networks. When folks ask me how to build their homes, I tell them to close their waste and supply loops on their own property: Manage your own sewage, obtain your own water, compost your own waste, and make your own energy. Build your house so it can either return to nature via a decomposition cycle or make its parts demountable and reusable for their next life. We demonstrate these principles in our farm infrastructure. This can work in the city as well, but only at certain densities. Manhattan's ultimate density is unsustainable. Many of the rust belt cities of the northern U.S. can handle their food production and waste systems at a neighborhood level. This, as well as village and rural networks, is where our future lies.

The importance of resiliency is plain as day. Every season is uncharacteristic. This winter is one of the coldest we have ever seen; last winter was one of the warmest. Ten years ago I remember driving to work in fifteen below zero temperatures a few mornings each year. This year the nights have been between five below zero and ten above zero for weeks straight. I do not know what is coming, but we are preparing for contingencies. This is resiliency. We wonder how large our firewood pile should be each year...our country should be wondering about its energy security as a whole. And it should not be reliant on the vagaries of tyrants in far off lands or the actions of our military. We need to take responsibility for our own energy future, on our own soil.

In the last two years I experienced painful change. I have presented this most profoundly in the allegory of dreams about a mansion, presented in three acts. My subconscious presented these dreams to me as I transformed. Only after writing this book did I realize the full meaning of the dreams.

The mansion was a model of my mind. In the first act, existing on the upper levels of the mansion referred to the abstract explorations of my professional life. Running through the corridors and opening the doors showed all I was discovering about changing the way we thought about the environment and about building, and the urgency I felt in conveying what I had seen to others. And my frustration in the realization that no one understood what I was seeing, without my stopping to lead them step by step through each realization.

In the second act, on the bottom floor of the mansion, my practical self dealt with what was visible in front of my eyes. It was my "flip" from abstract exploration to applied craft, but still utilizing the memories of what I had seen on the upper levels. Here I was content to draw inward, and reflect on the union of the abstract and the applied. It was my pulling inward after the trauma of professional life.

In the third act the mansion collapsed in a great storm, and a character called the medium knitted my two selves in the reconciliation of the abstract and practical. I became liberated by the destruction of all the objects I treasured on the upper floors of the mansion. This was my release of the baggage of my previous life, my realization that I was no longer an architect, and the preservation of my ego in my new life. What I carried within self-validated me; unified the poles of my personality.

NOW, I am a recursed passenger, on the spiral between the applied and the abstract. I love my life and my family in the now of our farm. I wonder if another flip will bring me back to theory in the next five or ten years, and in what field it will manifest itself. One thing is sure: I will never again let go of my place, my family, or my self in the future wanderings of my mind.

Author Biography

Peter Larson is a former architect who lives with his wife, Hilarie and their three children in Lansing, New York. They own Just a Few Acres farm, which produces broiler chickens, eggs, turkeys, beef, and pork. Peter is the seventh generation on his family's farm. He and his family aspire to live self sufficiently and produce healthy food for their community. They harvest their own power via solar electricity, their own heat via firewood harvested from their farm, and much of their own food via their livestock, gardens and orchard. More information on their farm can be found at justafewacres.com. Peter's writings on sustainability and architecture can be found at peterlarson.org.

Made in the USA
Middletown, DE
22 August 2021

46703463R00175